112 Ways to Succeed
in Any Negotiation or Mediation

Secrets from a Professional Mediator

Steven G. Mehta

AuthorHouse™
1663 Liberty Drive
Bloomington, IN 47403
www.authorhouse.com
Phone: 1-800-839-8640

©*2009 Steven G. Mehta. All rights reserved.*

No part of this book may be reproduced, stored in a retrieval system, or transmitted by any means without the written permission of the author.

First published by AuthorHouse 5/29/2009

ISBN: 978-1-4389-8393-6 (e)
ISBN: 978-1-4389-8392-9 (sc)
ISBN: 978-1-4389-8391-2 (hc)

Library of Congress Control Number: 2009904852

Printed in the United States of America
Bloomington, Indiana

This book is printed on acid-free paper.

PRAISE FOR THE BOOK

"Steve Mehta has taken a complex, multi-disciplinary approach to negotiation and has simplified it into component parts so that any person interested in the subject can understand."

-Jeffrey Krivis, Mediator and Author of
"Improvisational Negotiation - A Mediator's Stories of Conflict About Love, Money, Anger and the Strategies To Resolve Them"

"112 Ways…should be a part of any successful supervisor's human resource "survival kit." I found the chapter on negotiating styles to be particularly helpful in illustrating how we all play roles toward improving the communication process which can get the parties willing to compromise."

-Marc Herrera, Vice President, Skilled Nursing Administration and Risk Management, Southern California Presbyterian Homes

"Mehta deftly blends his personal experiences, with compelling historical cases, and respected experimental research. He displays sensitivity to and illuminates the hidden and unconscious elements of negotiation."

- Don Brownlee, Prof. of Communication Studies, California State University Northridge

"A terrific book which lays out numerous straightforward and practical strategies for successful negotiators. Mehta's work combines social science, real world experience and negotiation insights that will give you an extra edge in your future negotiations."

- Gig Kyriacou, Mediator

"Steve Mehta does an excellent job analyzing the psychologically complex and fascinating subject of negotiation. His anecdotal discussions drawing from his extensive experience as a trial lawyer and mediator make this book an interesting read. Steve provides practical approaches to negotiation that will benefit practitioners and lay people alike."

- Steve Cerveris, Mediator at Cerveris Mediation

"This thought provoking primer provides many interesting examples of negotiation's central importance in our lives. Thankfully, it is an easy read; simplifying an otherwise obtuse topic for everyone looking for that special edge."

-Mike Townsend, Vice President, Marketing,
Southern California Presbyterian Homes

"Effective negotiation and mediation skills are essential in many walks of life. A key element in developing and improving such skills is the confidence that is gained from experience. Steve Mehta shares with us in this book his extensive experience and in-depth knowledge of the subject. Both professional advisors and public representatives alike will find Mehta's book an invaluable tool when negotiating or mediating between parties who have, at the outset, seemingly intractable differences – and who are relying on their advisors or representatives to guide them towards a successful resolution."

- Councillor Jonathan Findlay, LLB (Hons) Dip. LP, NP –
Cabinet Member for Education,
Glasgow City Council, Glasgow, Scotland

"Mr. Mehta's book is an indispensable resource that belongs in every negotiator's toolbox. He clearly and succinctly describes every facet of negotiation -- from strategy and tactics to emotions and culture – to help you become a master negotiator."

- Eleanor Barr, Esq., Mediator at ADR Services, Inc

"Even though we do it, many times each and every day, most of us dislike the whole negotiation process, What Steve Mehta accomplishes in this book is to ease the reader thru all types of negotiations, from understanding the needs of all parties, and then developing strategies to maximize outcomes that are meaningful and sustainable. Adopting the steps contained in this book will give the reader a greater sense of successful problem solving, whether it be at home, in the market or in the boardroom."

- Cliff Hendler, President, Dispute Resolution Services LP, Toronto, Canada and Co-Founder of the International Academy of Mediators

"In a very practical way, Mr. Mehta outlines all the necessary steps to succeed in any negotiation from planning to executing while considering the emotional and communicative factors. Every day consumers to litigation attorneys will benefit from this well written guide by this experienced and successful mediator"

- Rosemarie Chiusano Drohan, Executive Vice President of Business Development, Judicate West

"The book lays out some very good precepts regarding how best to go about the process of negotiating with another party. While it may seem obvious, there are, in fact, basic ways to go about the process of negotiating. My one important take-away is that one needs to be very deliberate about how you negotiate and what you want to get from the negotiating process."

- Gregory D. Bearce, MBA, MAG, MDiv, Vice President, Operations, The Episcopal Home Communities

PRAISE FOR THE AUTHOR

"Mr. Mehta's efforts brought resolution to a case which I thought would not settle. Without a doubt, we would recommend him for future mediations."
—Steven Barkin - Stockdale & Wilson - Los Angeles, CA

"I wish to thank you once again for the excellent job you did in settling this case for us. Everyone involved is extremely grateful to you and very much impressed with your patience, attention to detail, homework, and ability to read character, all of which helped this case to settle."
—Victor Jacobovitz - Los Angeles, CA

"I handle complex personal-injury matters and have mediated numerous cases with some of California's best mediators. Without a doubt, Steve Mehta is ranked as one of the best mediators I have seen. He is professional, insightful, and will not stop working until the case is resolved. I would recommend him to anyone for their mediations."
—Gerald MacRae - Los Angeles, CA

"I want to personally thank you for the outstanding job you did in the dispute. It was without a doubt the best mediation session I have ever participated in. You were excellent. You were able to identify the issue, eliminate all the unnecessary baggage, and get each side to compromise to resolve the matter."
—Sue Ann Howard - Lancaster, CA

"I have attended numerous mediations. Mr. Mehta is one of the best mediators I have seen in any of those."
—Luis Soman - Los Angeles, CA

"This man is a miracle worker."
—Adam Silverstein - Carpenter & Zuckerman - Los Angeles, CA

"I don't know how you did it! You settled a case that was headed towards a long trial. Job well done, Mr. Mehta!"
—Morton Struhl - Inglewood, CA

"Before I came here to your mediation, I was convinced that we would have to try this case to have a resolution. After seeing Mr. Mehta work, I was convinced that he can mediate anything."
—Robert Kum - Los Angeles, CA

"From early on, you made us feel that we had hope that we could settle this case. Your positive outlook and your skill as a mediator helped guide us to settlement."
—David Ortega - Los Angeles, CA

"As a defense attorney, I have worked with many mediators. Mr. Mehta is one of the best mediators I have seen. He works hard to achieve a fair resolution for both sides. He took time and skill to get the job done despite vastly different starting points."
—Kenneth Ralidis - Los Angeles, CA

"Steve Mehta is one of the best mediators I have come across in a long time. He is extremely helpful with workable suggestions to move towards settlement."
—Elaine Trevino - Civil Service Employees - Pasadena, CA

"Mr. Mehta, without a doubt, is an extremely effective mediator. He was fair to both sides and helped settle a case that we had not been able to do for a very long time. He suggested several approaches that ultimately proved successful in bridging the gap between the parties. Mr. Mehta will be the first name I suggest."
—Robert French - Valencia, CA

"Steve is very creative in coming up with alternative approaches to mediating. He is a good listener and makes you feel 'heard.' He is very creative and knowledgeable as to what works."
—Julie Esposito - Prestholt & Fidone, LLP - Pasadena, CA

"There is no doubt, you are one of the best mediators I have ever seen."
—Lorenzo Taylor - State Farm Insurance - Thousand Oaks, CA

"Steven Mehta is the best mediator I have ever used. Every mediator must emulate his style. I don't think I will want to use another mediator over him."
—Chima Anyanwu - Los Angeles, CA

ACKNOWLEDGMENTS

I would like to thank my wife, Michele, for consistently helping me with ideas, moral support and for reviewing several versions of this book. Your graciousness when I woke you at 2 a.m. to discuss an idea was and is always appreciated. Without you, this book would never have been written.

I would also like to thank my son for giving me the inspiration to write so many different chapters of this book. Alex, you are a natural-born negotiator.

Thank you also to my parents for lovingly guiding me in all things.

I would like to thank Margaret Sparrow for being extremely patient with all my changes and edits.

Lisa Miller, this book wouldn't be the same without your careful and watchful eye.

I would like to also thank my friends, and you know who you are, for helping me come up with ideas, rewrites, and for proofreading my book.

Without all of you, this book would not be possible.

Thank you.

Contents

Praise for the Author	xi
Acknowledgments	xiii
Introduction	xxi

Before There Was A Negotiation, There Was The Negotiation About The Negotiation

Your History With An Opponent Will Affect The Way You Negotiate	3
The Other Side Expects To Negotiate	4
Before The Other Side Perceives A Negotiation, Spy On Their Intentions And Actions	5
Preparing For Lunch	7

Preparing For A Negotiation

Have A Game Plan	11
It's the Difference Between Chess And Checkers	13
Play Three-Dimensional Chess	14
Know Your Case	17
Know The Market	18
Understand Your Emotional Buttons And Know When They Are Being Pushed	19
Know What Motivates You and Your Opponent	21
Barriers To Effective Communication	23
Bring a Written Contract	25
Locate Mutual Friends	27
Rehearse, Rehearse, Rehearse	28
War-game The Negotiation	30
Possible Solutions	31
Know Your Alternatives	33

Perception Is Power	35
Bring Food and Drink	37
Location, Location, Location	38
Timing Is Everything	40

Negotiating Styles

Competitive Style	45
Cooperative Style	47
Pragmatic Style	49
Extroverted Style	50
Conflict-Avoidance Style	51
Analytical Problem-Solving Style	53
Amiable, Accommodating Style	55
Sensory Learners And Learning Styles	57
Age Considerations	59
Are You Hindering The Process?	61

Where To Start

Understand your Relationship with Your Opponent	65
The Greater Your Expectations, The Greater Your Chance Of Recovery	66
Negotiating Chips	68
Demonstrate Your Competence	70
The Less You Know About The Other Side, The More Optimistic Your Initial Position Should Be	71
Establish A Friendly Rapport With Your Opponent Early	73
Establish Initial Commitments	75
People Value Things Less If They Come From The Other Side	76
Don't Make An Offer Until You Are Ready	77
Who Has The Authority To Negotiate?	78

Consider Your Proposal From Your Opponent's Perspective	79
Acknowledge The Other Person's Problems Before Asking Them To Help You	80
Let The Other Side Underestimate Your Skills	82
Focus On The Few Good Points	84
Ask The Other Side To Commit To Something You Know Is Wrong (And Can Be Proven Wrong)	86

The Negotiation

Range Bargaining	91
What If…	92
How Much? Or, You Want *What*??	93
Make Two Offers	95
You'll Have To Do Better Than That	96
Don't Focus On Your Bottom Line	97
Maintain Limited Authority	100
Listen With A Goal In Mind	102
Be Silent	104
Be Patient	105
Good Cop/Bad Cop	107
Negotiate To The Other Side's Needs, Not To Yours	109
The (Limited) Power Of Norms	111
People Defer To Authority	112
If It's Important Enough To Do, Do It In Person	114
"Off The Record" Comments Are Always On The Record	116
Getting Angry Only Weakens Your Position	117
Anger By The Other Side Can Be A Means To Control You	119
A Picture Is Worth A Thousand Words	121
Say "I" And Not "You"	123
Deadline Do's and Don'ts	124

Demonstrate That The Other Side Has Something To Lose From Not Making The Deal	126
Help The Other Side Save Face	128
Incorporate The Other Side's Proposal In Your Counter	130
Care (But Not Too Much)	132
Be Careful About Splitting The Difference	133
In Good Conscience, I Must Say "No"	135
We've Never Done That Before	137
Ask Questions	138

Negotiating With A Client

Share Weaknesses And Strengths with Clients	143
Tap Into Your Sixth Sense	145
Have Your Client Argue for The Other Side	147
Never State That You Have Control Over Your Client	149
Separate The Client From The Representative	151
If Your Client Made A Mistake, Find A Scapegoat	153
Preview The Process For Your Client	155
Make The Other Side's Representative Look Good	157
Give The Representative Talking Points To Justify Their Recommendations to the Client	159

Using A Neutral Mediator

You Both Must Have Trust In The Mediator	163
Help the Mediator Understand Your Side	165
Have The Mediator Suggest Your Offer	167
Inform The Mediator Of Any Special Needs	168
Consider Asking The Mediator To Make A "Mediator's Proposal"	170
Ask The Mediator Questions	172
Ask For The Mediator's Recommendations	173

Let The Mediator Explain The Reality of the situation To Your Client	174
Should You Reveal A Bottom Line To The Mediator?	175

A Little Bit More

Ask For Something Not Directly Related To The Negotiation	179
Put It In Writing	181
Modify Minor Provisions Such As Delivery Or Date Of Payment	183
Explain That You Need It Because…	185

The After-Party

Have Them Participate In Writing It Down	189
Writing (As Opposed To Filling In Blanks)	190
Create A Checklist For Others To Follow	191

Ten Common Mistakes Made In Negotiation And Mediation

Mediating Or Negotiating Too Early Or Too Late	195
Discussing Terms And Dollars Too Soon	196
Refusing To Concede The Obvious	198
Believing That Your Wishes Will Change Their Actions	200
Demanding Total Capitulation	201
Negotiating and Mediating Without The Necessary Parties	203
Not Getting It In Writing	204
Rushing The Process; Being Impatient	206
Assuming "This Is My Final Offer" Really Is The Final Offer	208
Talking Too Much	209
About The Author	211
Additional Reading And Resources	213

INTRODUCTION

Everybody negotiates! From the child on the playground to the lawyer in the courtroom, everybody negotiates at some time. Even the people who say they don't like to negotiate are negotiating. The simple fact is that negotiations affect every aspect of our lives.

Children, and certainly my son, seem to be born to negotiate. They know how to negotiate bedtime, a little more television, a little less broccoli, and so many other things. But there is so much more to negotiating than the simple tools we learned as children. In fact, negotiations can be very sophisticated depending on the situation. Yet at the same time, negotiations can be very simple. Negotiations primarily depend on using the right tools at the right time.

Luckily, you don't have to be a rocket scientist to be a good negotiator. In fact, being a rocket scientist might make you a worse negotiator because they may complicate matters unnecessarily by over-thinking the problem. (no offense to rocket scientists, including my sister-in-law, who happens to be one). Negotiating well can be very easily accomplished. You only have to keep in mind a few simple concepts:

- The nature of the negotiation is affected by the relationship with the other person.
- Each side's interests are more important than each side's positions.
- In negotiations, just as in life, the little things often count more than the big things.
- No matter what you do, you cannot convince another person to do things for your reasons. You must convince people to do things based upon their own reasons.

- There is no magic technique or trick that will make people do things in negotiations.

This book is designed to provide you with the tools and techniques that will help you negotiate better in all situations. There are many different techniques. Not every technique will be useful in every situation. However, these techniques will provide you with ways to handle most negotiating situations. Finding out which technique works in which situation will probably require some experimentation on your part.

This book is divided into stages of negotiations. Each stage contains different things that can and will happen, and each section is designed to provide specific techniques that may apply in that particular stage of negotiation.

It is helpful to think of negotiations like a game. One of the best game examples that compares to negotiation is the game of chess. Chess requires planning, strategy, execution, and follow up. The same is true of negotiations. In life, the negotiators are the chess pieces. Usually, in negotiations, just as in chess, a team is required to win the game. As such, you will see some chess related themes throughout the book.

Finally, becoming a successful negotiator requires you to practice your craft. Exercise the new skills you learn in this book—go to swap meets, and take joy in negotiating over a product. Go to a department store and see if you can get a discount. Try some techniques on your family and friends.

The more you practice these skills, the more you will find that certain techniques work better in some situations than in others.

Happy negotiating!

BEFORE THERE WAS A NEGOTIATION, THERE WAS THE NEGOTIATION ABOUT THE NEGOTIATION

One of the critical things affecting an ongoing negotiation are the actions that have taken place *before* the negotiation. This section will focus on past activities, actions, and events that can affect how the negotiation will proceed.

YOUR HISTORY WITH AN OPPONENT WILL AFFECT THE WAY YOU NEGOTIATE

Many negotiations involve parties that have had earlier interactions with each other. With those prior interactions come history and baggage. Your negotiating opponent will have his or her own perception of that history. It is important to understand that your history with the opponent will affect the way you negotiate.

An example: If you are a salesperson negotiating a commission for a sale, and in your last interaction with your negotiating partner that person cheated you out of your commission. How would you approach that person when the time comes to negotiate a new deal? You would likely be more distrustful. You would probably double-check the numbers and terms to make sure you are not being cheated this time around. On the other hand, if in your prior interaction the other person was very detailed and made sure to properly account for your commission, your interaction would be quite different. As the famous saying goes, "Fool me once, shame on you; fool me twice, shame on me."

When conducting any interactions or negotiations with anyone, it is, therefore, very important that you consider how your actions today will affect your future interactions with this person. Are you burning a bridge or building one?

THE OTHER SIDE EXPECTS TO NEGOTIATE

Many people are afraid to negotiate. They are concerned about how the other side will perceive them if they start to negotiate. Generally, however, the other side expects to negotiate. Even in the United States, where people don't usually negotiate or haggle over daily items, there is a considerable amount of daily negotiating.

Generally, the larger the item or the greater the risk, the greater the chance that the other side expects to negotiate. Even regarding everyday staples the other side expects some form of negotiation. For instance, most people believe that a grocery store doesn't negotiate. But every Sunday paper is full of negotiations—ads from various stores quoting their mottos ("Everyday low prices") or special prices or a sale on milk or the phrase "We will match any competitor's advertised price."

If you ask to negotiate, all the other side needs to say is "no." And you don't even have to accept that answer; sometimes a "no" is the beginning of a negotiation.

BEFORE THE OTHER SIDE PERCEIVES A NEGOTIATION, SPY ON THEIR INTENTIONS AND ACTIONS

In most negotiations, the moment you start interacting, and sometimes even before you meet with the other side, you are involved in negotiations. The trick is to realize this fact before the other side does; you can then investigate and discover as much information as possible without the other side being aware that you are investigating.

Most people find that information acquired independently, before the other side expects to share information, is more credible than information shared when motivated by a negotiation or sale.

For example, many employers conduct background checks on prospective employees. Some employers investigate prospective employees on such websites as Facebook, MySpace, and LinkedIn to find out more about the applicant before he or she ever arrives for an interview. The reason is that the employer can learn more about the person from the unfiltered pre-interview information than from statements during the interview.

In an example from a different context, James was claiming during a mediation that a brawl was started by Devon and Todd, the defendants, and that he was not drunk at the time of the incident, and moreover, that he, James, rarely drank in public. In a deposition, after the lawsuit was filed, he persisted in telling the same story. However, his MySpace page was full of pictures showing him at fraternity parties, drinking large quantities of alcohol, making threats of violence against others, and generally acting in a manner inconsistent with his statements.

Similarly, in the international spy business, intelligence on other countries that is secretly obtained is more valuable than the information presented in public propaganda.

So it is in the negotiations business.

PREPARING FOR LUNCH

Most people don't think about using a lunch or coffee break as an opportunity to enhance negotiations. The truth is that having lunch or coffee with someone can create a bond that will serve you well in future negotiations. In addition to the lunch itself, however, an inexpensive way to increase your negotiating position is to pick up the tab afterwards.

Buying lunch or coffee for your opponent takes advantage of the psychological principle of reciprocity. In his book *Influence: Science and Practice*, social scientist Robert Cialdini identified the principle of reciprocity as follows: People are more likely to do something nice for you if you have already done something nice for them. In other words, "if you scratch my back, I'll scratch yours."

Cialdini referred to a study investigating whether free gifts can affect the number of sales of raffle tickets. The study found that if the salesperson voluntarily and without prompting gave the subjects a soda, those subjects were much more likely to buy tickets. Reciprocity is a powerful tool that can be used during negotiations.

Buying lunch for your opponent starts your negotiation off on the right foot before any terms are ever offered. Your nice deed can pay dividends at the negotiating table.

PREPARING FOR A NEGOTIATION

Preparation and hard work are the keys to success for many activities, including negotiations.

Sufficient preparation can mean the difference between striking a good bargain and striking a great bargain. In fact, studies have shown that good negotiators prepare four times as much as average negotiators. Remember, success comes when preparation meets opportunity.

This section focuses on how to prepare for a negotiation, and what is necessary as a precursor to negotiation.

HAVE A GAME PLAN

Probably the most important factor when preparing for a negotiation is to have a game plan. Without that game plan, you will not be able to evaluate whether you have a good deal. As the famous Chinese philosopher Sun Tzu said, "All battles are won *before* they are fought."

In fact, negotiation researchers have found that there should be a 9:1 ratio for the amount of time preparing for a negotiation versus the amount of time spent in the negotiation process. Unfortunately, for many negotiators that ratio is reversed, with much too little time spent on preparation. To quote Benjamin Franklin, "By failing to plan, you are failing to prepare."

A good game plan outlines the steps necessary to arrive at a negotiation and what steps you will take during the negotiation. The plan should identify your objectives and goals and allow you to evaluate your strengths and weaknesses as well as that of your position so that you are able to identify and seize opportunities when they arise.

If you can, try to chart or graph your game plan. It is helpful to have visual reminders and cues to assist you in your planning, and a chart will give you the flexibility to adjust to changing situations as the negotiations proceed.

The following sample topics may help you get started with your game plan:

- Goal/objective: Identify what your goal or objective is in a few sentences.

- o What is the problem that needs to be solved?
- o What are the needs of the other side?
- o What are your needs?
- o What approaches have worked in prior situations?
- Time frame: What is the time frame for your project/negotiation?
- Pre-negotiation to-do list: What needs to be done in preparation for the negotiation, and how much time is to be allocated to these items?
  - o Identify each item separately, and specify the timeline for each.
- Is there any background on this project or the customer/client?
- What advantages are there for your opponent to working or negotiating with you?
- What position or situation will you be in when you commence negotiations?
- What strategies will be useful for the negotiation?

The game plan gives you the direction and road map necessary for properly negotiating a successful deal.

IT'S THE DIFFERENCE BETWEEN CHESS AND CHECKERS

Both chess and checkers are excellent games. Most people, however, understand that chess requires the player to strategize and think ahead. Many chess masters think three, four or more moves ahead. The same holds true for negotiations. It is important to consider what the other side will do three and four moves out.

Negotiation, by its nature, is a constant flux involving two or more parties with different needs trying to find a mutually acceptable resolution. Most negotiations require many different steps. A home purchase is one example. It starts with offers and counteroffers, but even when a price is agreed upon, the deal doesn't end there. There are still other moves to be negotiated, such as the escrow timeline, the repairs (if necessary), the deposit, and many other items.

By planning ahead and anticipating what the other side will do in response to your negotiating position, you will be in a better position to arrive at the most advantageous solution.

PLAY THREE-DIMENSIONAL CHESS

In negotiations, it is necessary to think ahead on many levels like in the game of Three Dimensional Chess. The game of Three Dimensional Chess or Tri-Dimensional Chess was developed in the 18th century, but came into public light by the television series Star Trek. The game has three chess boards, each layered above the other in vertical alignment. A player can make a move on both a horizontal field of play as well as a vertical field. A player can move in all directions: Up, down, left, right, forward or backwards.

Just as in Tri-Dimensional Chess, thinking several moves ahead of your opponent should not be limited to the tactical arena of negotiations. It is equally important to realize that in every negotiation, several elements of communication are at play: The actual content of the communication, the personal philosophy or worldview that your counterpart imposes into the communication, and the emotions that each side brings to the negotiation. Each factor has its own unique problems and issues, and in order for the negotiation to be successful, each factor must be carefully evaluated and thought through.

Before you make the initial offer, determine not only what the objective meaning of that offer will be but also what emotions, history, and background you inject into the negotiation. While you may assign a certain meaning to your offer, there are no guarantees that the other side will infer the same meaning from it. Will they interpret your gesture as something other than what you intended? If so, how will that skew your message? By the way, if you can't answer these questions, then you haven't fully evaluated the issue, because these things happen in every interaction.

A recent case where multiple dimensions had to be addressed involved the purchase of a restaurant business between two parties from an Asian country. The buyers, Mr. Khan and his business partner, orally agreed to purchase the restaurant from the seller, Mr. Patel, and neither party put anything down in writing. The agreement was made with a handshake and the exchange of $101 as a down payment. The buyers later claimed that the purchase price was $1.2 million, and the seller stated that the price was $1.5 million.

The buyers took over the premises and started working in the restaurant. They had made multiple payments of several hundred thousand dollars each to the seller, when the issue of the price arose. The two parties disagreed on the price but agreed to mediation to try to resolve the issues. Several questions had to be addressed during the mediation: First, there was the strict dollar issue. What was the evidence of the agreed-upon price?

The parties then started to negotiate the terms of the price. In essence, they started to renegotiate the price.

In some sense, the renegotiation happened on a different level and had a second, cultural, dimension. Specifically, most people raised in the Western world would view this new discussion of price as an unacceptable breach of the original agreement. In Mr. Khan and Mr. Patel's culture, however, it was viewed simply as an acceptable renegotiation.

A third dimension that had to be addressed was rooted within the two men's culture itself and in the meaning attributed to actions that were an expression of that culture: Mr. Khan viewed the initial exchange of $101 as a meaningful statement of intent and as a gesture of good faith, allowing for prosperity on both sides, and he felt that Mr. Patel had violated that cultural belief and was, therefore, not acting in good faith. Because the parties could never agree on the price, each believed the other violated the good faith requirement implied by the $101 transaction.

A fourth dimension was the operation of the business. Mr. Khan and his partner had invested an enormous amount of money since taking over the restaurant. If they simply walked away from the deal and the business, they would likely lose their money, and the business would fall apart. But if they continued to operate the business, they would be benefiting Mr. Patel alone in case they had to give the business back.

A fifth dimension was that Mr. Khan, a chef, was Mr. Patel's former employee. Mr. Patel looked down on Mr. Khan as being of a lower socioeconomic status. Mr. Khan, on the other hand, viewed himself as Mr. Patel's equal and would have been insulted to learn that he was considered beneath Mr. Patel.

The last dimension that affected the negotiations was how the two parties' particular cultural sensitivities would be judged by a Western jury in the case of a trial—a jury that had no understanding of those issues. The jury would ultimately decide the case based on its own cultural standards.

All of these factors had to be considered and evaluated as part of every move during the negotiations. Instead of three-dimensional chess, it was more like six-dimensional chess.

Even when people think that they are saying and hearing the same thing, that may not be the case. The emotional charge associated with a comment may be different depending on who says it and who hears it. That emotional component adds yet another dimension to the negotiation that must be addressed. You should try to consciously minimize any emotional overtones that are not necessary to communicating raw data.

Newton's Third Law of Motion is that for every action, there is a reaction. By recognizing that each negotiating move involves multiple levels and dimensions, and that participants may have different reactions on different levels, you will be in a better position to handle the complexities of any negotiation.

KNOW YOUR CASE

Before you ever enter a negotiation, know the strengths and weaknesses of your position. The last thing you want is to learn about a flaw in your case for the first time during a negotiation or mediation.

When I am in mediation, after having reviewed the facts, I often make a comment about a fact or weakness that could affect a particular side's negotiating position. Good negotiators are prepared for such comments and can show me and the other side that they are not only aware of the issue but that they have made certain allowances in their negotiating position because of it.

Knowing your case requires you to unblinkingly evaluate your situation. You have to be willing to ask the hard questions: Why is your product or service better? In what ways is it unique? What do neutral or independent parties have to say about your product? Why does your opponent need to negotiate with you? How long can you last without making a deal?

Failing to ask yourself these types of questions means you cannot fully understand your position's strengths and weaknesses. But by answering them you will surely strengthen your negotiating position and appear more credible.

KNOW THE MARKET

The importance of knowing the relevant market conditions is something real estate agents have recognized for a long time. If you're planning to buy a home in an up market, agents tell you to adjust your price upward; if you're selling in a down market, agents tell you to adjust your price downward. Knowing market forces and conditions seems intuitive in the context of real estate or the stock market, but in fact market conditions affect every business.

Factors such as timing, competition, resources, emotional appeals, attitudes of prospective buyers, etc., affect any negotiation. To fully prepare, it is critical that you understand the market conditions that apply to your specific situation.

For example, in lawsuits, the way juries are expected to react to certain cases affects the value of settlements. If juries have awarded large sums for certain type of cases, the settlements for those cases will became larger. On the other hand, if the verdicts are smaller or the defense tends to win more of those types of cases, the negotiated settlements will become smaller

Getting to know the market conditions can be very simple. Internet search engines can help you with your research; you can review periodicals and literature; you can consult with experts in the field. There is no wrong way to learn about the market. The key is to make the effort to learn all that you can to maximize your negotiation results.

UNDERSTAND YOUR EMOTIONAL BUTTONS AND KNOW WHEN THEY ARE BEING PUSHED

Everything we do in life can create an emotional trigger for somebody, and emotions are a very real part of negotiations. Understanding what triggers your emotional reactions is critical to successful negotiations. If you understand your own buttons, you will be better prepared to address them when they are being pushed. And knowing that you have them helps you understand what creates emotional triggers in others.

Emotional triggers are events, actions, personality types, or things that cause an intense emotional response. Common emotional triggers during negotiations are your opponent's demonstration of anger, unreasonable offers, blatant incompetence, time wasting, arrogance or inflated egos, and verbal attacks. All these behaviors are frustrating to pretty much anyone during negotiations. But the question is not whether they are frustrating but whether they trigger an intense emotional reaction in you.

For example, in the movie *The Godfather*, an assassination attempt is made on Vito Corleone, the Godfather. His oldest son, Sonny, is outraged and immediately wants to react by attacking the enemy with guns blazing. Sonny is responding to an emotional trigger; he's angry and reacts in anger. Michael, the youngest son, is also angry at the attempt on his father's life, but he tries to respond logically and rationally; he assumes—correctly—that their enemies would probably expect them to react with guns blazing. He is able to recognize the emotional trigger and control it.

Once you know what your triggers are, you can take steps to control them. You can catch yourself before you react emotionally to a trigger and instead respond with emotional intelligence.

In one particular negotiation, a party reacted emotionally because it felt disrespected by the other side. After I explained to each side the issues involved with those feelings of disrespect, we were able to arrive at a solution that demonstrated respect for one party, while still maintaining the interests of the other.

Emotional triggers can negatively affect a negotiation. Understanding them and controlling them before a negotiation can be crucial to success.

KNOW WHAT MOTIVATES YOU AND YOUR OPPONENT

Every person who enters a negotiation is motivated by something different, and those motivations must be satisfied.

Understanding what motivates people in negotiations has several benefits. First, the more you know about what motivates your opponent, the more you know about what may threaten him or her. Ever since the stone ages, humans have displayed a fight-or-flight instinct in response to threats, and thousands of years of evolution later, modern humans still have the same reaction to perceived or real threats. If someone or something threatens them or their egos, they either fight (and argue) or they withdraw from the aggressor. In fact, according to some researchers, anger is merely your body's defense mechanism kicking in.

Sometimes negotiations go awry because someone inadvertently threatens the opponent's worldview or ego, triggering the fight-or-flight reaction and causing that person to become defensive. The result of having two people involved in a negotiation that both exhibit defensive behavior is usually quite bad. This is because people acting in defensive postures aren't able to rationally solve problems. Understanding the other side's motivations can help avoid the problem and prevent the defensiveness.

The other advantage of understanding your opponent's motivations is the ability to identify mutually advantageous solutions. Take the classic situation of the mother faced with two daughters who each want the last orange. Not wanting to disappoint either daughter, the mother inquires as to why each girl wants the orange. One daughter responds that she wants to eat the fruit. The other says she wants it for the peel so that she can bake. By understanding each daughter's motivation, the mother is able to arrive at a win-win solution by giving the fruit to one daughter and the peel to the other.

A British study found that effective negotiators spent 400 percent more time evaluating the common interests and concerns of their opponents than did average negotiators. The same study also showed that effective negotiators spent double the time obtaining information—in terms of understanding positions and clarifying issues—than did average negotiators.

Before commencing negotiations, make sure you understand everyone's motivations.

BARRIERS TO EFFECTIVE COMMUNICATION

One of the most common problems in negotiations is that people do not properly communicate with each other. A common complaint in mediations and disputes is that the other side "just doesn't understand." One of the primary reasons for this lack of understanding is that everyone has certain common barriers to effective communication. Understanding and eliminating those barriers is a crucial first step to effective negotiating.

Everyone has filters through which they perceive the world. Those filters help us cope with the daily onslaught of information and make decisions quickly and efficiently. For example, when people are speaking, we filter that information through a language filter, or barrier. If the words are in a different language, we cannot understand the message. When the interpreter translates those words, we have a better understanding of what the other side is saying. However, with any translation, there is a slight, and in some cases significant, loss of meaning.

There are numerous barriers, or filters, to communication. Some of the common ones are physical or environmental barriers, emotional or attitude barriers, cultural barriers, or language barriers.

In one case I dealt with, numerous communication barriers had to be overcome. An American woman was suing a Korean company for wage and hour violations. Some of the barriers in the resulting negotiation included a cultural barrier, a gender barrier between a female employee and male supervisors, a language barrier because neither side spoke the other's native tongue fluently, a physical barrier because neither side wanted to mediate at the other's place of business, and an emotional barrier because each side felt that the other had violated a trust. Every one of those barriers affected how each party understood the events that occurred during negotiations.

By understanding the type of barrier that could influence a decision, you will be better prepared to address those barriers when the negotiation takes place.

BRING A WRITTEN CONTRACT

No matter how far apart the parties are, or how early in the negotiations it is, always bring a written contract. If for some reason the other side suddenly wants to do the deal, you need to be prepared to capitalize on that opportunity and have the contract ready. If you don't know what the terms of the contract will be, bring something that allows you to write up the contract immediately. By "contract" I mean a written document that each person can sign and that captures the important terms of the deal. It doesn't have to be beautiful; it just has to be clear in describing what's important to you.

Written contracts are invaluable for several reasons. First, oral contracts, although legally enforceable in theory, are very difficult to prove. If there is a dispute over the terms of the contract, it will inevitably come down to a "he said, she said" standoff. Any agreement you enter into is worth putting in writing. In legal cases involving contracts or agreements, a written document demonstrating the contract invariably increases a party's chances of winning.

Second, by putting the terms of the agreement in writing, you are further committing the parties to the process and are that much closer to finalizing a deal. The more an opponent is committed to the negotiation, the greater your chances of entering into a deal—people don't like to quit something when they have invested substantial time and energy into it.

Third, too many deals have fallen through because of "buyer's remorse." For example, after an arduous negotiation about the amount an insurance company was going to pay its clients for their home, which had burned down, the homeowners finally agreed to a price. As soon as they left the building, they started to think that they could have done better at trial. Prior to the parties' leaving, I had insisted that they confirm the terms in writing—which turned out to be the only thing that kept the deal together.

A sad example of failing to bring the contract occurs in the movie *Jerry Maguire*. Jerry is a sports agent who has lost all his clients, including his biggest client, a quarterback and number-one draft pick. He travels to the quarterback's house, trying to win him back—successfully, as it turns out. Both Jerry and the client happily shake on the deal, and Jerry leaves, exhilarated that his superstar client is still with him. Several weeks later, when Jerry and his quarterback go to the draft, Jerry learns that his client has changed his mind and is about to sign with a competitor. He asks the client for something in writing, but the client refuses, stating that he's just "signed" with a competitor "an hour ago." As a result, Jerry loses the client, along with a huge commission.

If Jerry had brought a written contract with him when he went to the quarterback's house, or had insisted on something informal in writing, he would be better off. Not only would he have something binding, but the client would be more committed to the deal. Jerry learns the price of not being prepared only after the damage has been done.

LOCATE MUTUAL FRIENDS

Before the negotiations take place, find out as much as you can about your opponent and his or her product or position. Find out as much as possible about the other person's friends and locate any friends you have in common.

First, just as the old saying goes, you can judge a person by the company they keep. Finding out about your opponent's friends can provide important clues about his or her character, likes, and dislikes.

Second, studies have shown that people who like each other or have some form of relationship are less likely to engage in competitive negotiating strategies, where one wins and the other loses. Finding people you and your negotiating partner have in common changes the other side's perception of you.

For example, if your opponent finds out that several of his close friends and acquaintances are friends of yours, he will probably give your statements more consideration, knowing that his friends, whom he respects, respect you. And on the other hand, how would you react if your best friend said, "I would like to introduce you to a friend of mine who may be able to help your business. Do you mind if we meet with her?" The reality is, any friend of my friend's is a friend of mine.

Many people will be more inclined to make a particular decision if they know that several of their close friends have made a similar decision.

By letting your negotiating partner know that his friends have already accepted you as trustworthy, you can gain a significant advantage in getting him to lower his guard, and giving you an opportunity to strike a deal.

REHEARSE, REHEARSE, REHEARSE

Actors don't simply walk onto the stage and start a monologue—they rehearse. Negotiations are no different. It is important to rehearse what you are going to say, how you are going to say it, and when you are going to say it. If multiple people are part of the negotiation, it is important to rehearse each person's role.

Rehearsing provides many advantages in your negotiation. First, it will help you get over the jitters you may have when going into a new situation or making a big presentation. In fact, recent studies have shown that people who mentally and physically rehearse an activity are better able to execute it than people who only rehearse physically.

I have done these mental rehearsals many times. For example, when preparing for a big negotiation, I will plan in my head the phrases or concepts I am going to express. Every time I give a speech to an audience, I do a mental rehearsal of the entire speech.

Indeed, the U.S. Army has practiced this philosophy of rehearsal since the Vietnam War, when it found that placing soldiers into tactical situations as close as possible to the real thing helped cut down on unnecessary casualties and mistakes due to inexperience. The Army believes it is better to make the mistake in an exercise than on the battlefield. So, too, as a negotiator, it is better to make your mistakes in a rehearsal than during the actual negotiation.

In the real world of negotiations, you are sometimes forced into a position where you either cannot reveal the whole truth or have to avoid answering some hard-hitting questions. On other occasions, you might have to argue a point you don't truly believe in but have been ordered to represent. In some sense, your communication with the other side may involve some form of deception regarding a critical issue, such as the true nature of your bottom line. By practicing what you are going to say and how you will say it, you can avoid those tricky issues.

For example, you are in a highly competitive and heated litigation case involving an environmental cleanup that will cost your company millions of dollars. Every penny your client pays for the cleanup comes directly out of its bottom line. You have been given orders to save every penny possible but have authority to pay up to one million dollars. At the beginning of the negotiations, the other side says, "We can do the cleanup for $950,000. We would be willing to consider a lower number. What is the maximum amount you can afford to pay?" How do you respond? Do you simply say, "We can afford a million?" Or do you instead say something different?

You say something different. That something different is what you must rehearse.

No star athlete's or superstar actor's performance has ever been successful without rehearsals. As a superstar negotiator, what will you do?

WAR-GAME THE NEGOTIATION

Good military commanders know the value of war-gaming. In a war game, two commanders take opposite sides and conduct simulated warfare on a game board. The military has used intense war-game events for decades, where all the generals are brought together to war-game certain tactical scenarios. For example, in World War II, German generals conducted extensive war games to analyze where the allies were going to launch their attack on D-Day.

Most lawyers know the value of a good mock trial. Mock trials allow them to present theories, arguments, and facts and let the mock jurors evaluate which are the most convincing. Advertisers will assemble focus groups for new products to test their marketing strategies. The same principle applies in negotiations. By war-gaming or conducting a focus group for the negotiation, you can see how the other side might react to your specific claim or argument. And you can see how you will react when the other side makes a particular claim.

Through war-gaming, military commanders hope to see where their own weaknesses as well as those of their enemies lie. The same process must be used before every negotiation. By taking your strategy to its logical conclusion, you can determine whether there will be any major obstacles between you and your best possible result.

In one negotiation, I was asked to help a friend negotiate a large transaction. Over dinner, we talked about strategies and tactics as well as the different moves he and the other side could make. I played the role of the opponent. It turned out that during the war game, we predicted the exact moves the other side ended up making. He was well prepared for the negotiation and brokered a great deal.

POSSIBLE SOLUTIONS

Every negotiation requires the parties to brainstorm solutions. There is a specific methodology that is necessary for good brainstorming. Regardless of whether you are doing it with a team or individually, the key to brainstorming is to let your mind run free and list every single solution that you arrive at, without regard for feasibility. This process allows a free flow of thought and uninhibited creativity. There is always time to eliminate ideas that don't work, but you can't eliminate what wasn't there in the first place.

In a recent negotiation involving theft of business property, both sides of the dispute claimed that the other side was at fault and that the other side had several pieces of the property in question. The dispute had lasted for more than five years and was very heated. There did not appear to be any solution in sight—while both attorneys wanted resolution for their clients, neither wanted to show weakness. Eventually, the attorneys for both sides got together, with me as the neutral mediator, and I suggested that both parties brainstorm a solution. As noted above, the only rule for the brainstorming session was that no idea, regardless of how absurd, could be ruled out instantly. Every idea was written down and then evaluated.

During this process, the parties suggested a solution where each side would immediately inspect the other's property to determine if the goods in question were there. If anything was found, the party in possession would have a point counted against it. The more points each party accumulated, the more money it was required to pay the other side. Eventually, the parties determined that the idea was unworkable, but the process let each party see that there could be a solution if they worked together. And it reminded them that each side was losing money while the dispute raged.

This first step, brainstorming together, was the closest the parties had come to an agreement in many years. This small step allowed them to brainstorm other ideas, and eventually, through further mediation, they arrived at a solution to their longstanding dispute.

Brainstorming, if done right, can be a great platform from which to generate solutions.

KNOW YOUR ALTERNATIVES

Many people make the critical mistake in negotiations of failing to fully evaluate the options to a negotiated solution. Without knowing your alternatives, you are negotiating in a vacuum.

Many retailers rely on the fact that consumers do not properly evaluate their alternatives before making a purchase. They do this, for instance, by making the bold statement that they will "match or beat any competitor's price" and hope that you will simply believe they have the lowest prices. They hope that because of their bold statement you will perceive their price to be the lowest, when in actuality, they are simply trying to keep you from looking at your alternatives.

Recently, I purchased a new dishwasher from a retail store that had a similar "match or beat" price guarantee. Their price for the dishwasher turned out to be nearly twice as high as a competitor's. When I demonstrated this to the store manager, he grudgingly accepted the reduced price. That price reduction, however, would not have happened if I did not know my alternatives.

Many negotiators know this concept as "BATNA" (best alternative to a negotiated agreement) a term coined by negotiation researchers Roger Fisher and William Ury of Harvard University in their groundbreaking book *Getting to Yes*.

Negotiators must prepare for the negotiation by evaluating their BATNA. They must understand what would happen if no agreement was struck. In the case of my dishwasher, I knew that if I did not arrange a deal with this retailer, I could simply purchase my dishwasher from the other retailer for less money.

The BATNA helps you understand your strengths and weaknesses. Just as the sage advice goes, "Don't put all your eggs in one basket," don't assume that your only option is through the current negotiation. You always have choices.

PERCEPTION IS POWER

Every negotiation balances the needs of one side against the respective power of the other. If one side's needs are high but its power is low, it will not be able to meet its needs as easily as if it had greater power. Necessarily, the amount of power one has will affect the outcome of the negotiation. Negotiators must recognize the balance of power and learn how to change that balance to their advantage. The trick to this balance of power is understanding that everyone who negotiates has power and that power, in turn, is based upon perception.

The perception of power plays a role in every type of negotiation, from the simple sale to the complex political negotiation. The item, product, or service may remain the same, but the perception of it can change. Advertisers try to manipulate perceptions to influence consumers' purchasing decisions. For example, many infomercials state at the end of the presentation that "only the first 30 callers will get this special deal," or they urge the viewer to "hurry now because we can't give this deal much longer." Other advertisers will claim that "space is limited." Each of these claims is an attempt by advertisers to change your perception of your need for their products.

Researchers have found that people will react differently to a product or situation if they feel that they are in competition for it. For example, in 1973 the major television networks got into a bidding war over the television rights to the first showing of the movie *The Poseidon Adventure*. Ultimately, ABC agreed to pay $3.3 million for a single showing of the movie, which was far more than had been paid for any other network movie purchase at the time. In fact, ABC ultimately lost close to $1 million on the deal. The reason for the gigantic price was the networks' perception of the value of the movie, which was affected considerably by the competition for it. This was the first time that the three networks were forced to buy rights by means of an open-bid auction. The movie was the same, yet the value of it changed considerably due to the potential buyers' perceptions.

There are several sources of power. There is power arising from need, options, time, scarcity, competition, credibility, knowledge, and skills, among other things.

For example, if there is only one gas station in your city, how much power does that station possess, and why? Is it because of the consumers' need for gasoline? Is it because of the lack of competition that could force a lower price? Or perhaps a combination of reasons? Now, what if there are 100 gas stations, but one station's prices are always lower? How does that change the source of power?

Understanding what the perception of power is and where it comes from is a powerful way of preparing for negotiation

BRING FOOD AND DRINK

Oftentimes, people overlook their physical needs during a negotiation. Anytime you are negotiating, whether in an office, conference room, or other arena, make sure there is plenty of food and water to sustain you.

Most people come to a negotiation with the hope that it will be over quickly. Indeed, you often hear people say things like "I hope we can get this done soon," or "Let's get to the point," or "I don't like to beat around the bush." What most people don't realize is that negotiations generally *don't* proceed quickly. In negotiations, people don't get rewarded for being the first to simply make a deal; they are rewarded for making a good deal.

Reflect on some of your prior outings to the car dealership. You walk in at 10:00 a.m. and leave at 5:00 p.m. with a car. You may have missed breakfast that morning, so the last time you ate was 7:00 p.m. the night before. By the time you get to the important part of the negotiation at 4:00 p.m., you have gone close to 24 hours without any food, the only sustenance the dealership offers being coffee and popcorn.

If before you started your negotiation you had decided to pack a lunch to negotiate, you might have thought yourself crazy. However, at 4:00 p.m. all you can think about is how to get the deal done so you can get something to eat! The dealership now has the edge over you because they know that the longer they delay, the hungrier and more desperate you get. On the other hand, if you had brought food, your decision would no longer be governed by your empty stomach but by your pocketbook.

LOCATION, LOCATION, LOCATION

Where you conduct the negotiation can be just as important as how and when you conduct the negotiation.

Many factors decide where the negotiation will take place. Some of those factors may include avoiding a conflict by picking a neutral location or accepting the other side's location, time or convenience of the parties, cultural issues, and resources.

Some negotiators believe that a neutral location is imperative, and there are indeed many advantages to this, especially when strong egos are involved or neither side feels comfortable in the other's space. In many cases, the parties therefore insist that the mediation take place at the mediator's neutral office, to avoid unfair advantage.

But a neutral location may not always be the best choice, and the issue deserves analysis well ahead of the actual negotiation.

Negotiating at the opponent's location has advantages and drawbacks. For example, some people are less likely to prepare when they are on their home turf. In addition, people are generally more likely to have interruptions in their own space. This can be good or bad, depending on the situation.

One time I conducted a mediation at another lawyer's office. The lawyer was constantly taking calls, and his staff interrupted every 10 minutes. Finally, his client, who was worried about the deal falling apart said, "Today is about me, not your other cases! Concentrate on the task at hand!"

When the negotiation takes place at your location, you can't walk away from it, but the other side can. And when you are at your opponent's location, you can conduct some investigation—overhear conversations, possibly see documents, observe working patterns, and be exposed to potentially sensitive materials. On the other hand, the other side has more eyes and ears to observe you and your side.

In one case, the mediation was conducted at the plaintiff's attorney's office. The office was a shambles. There was very little conference room space, and the employees were practically in each other's laps. The other side's counsel noted the surroundings and inferred that he could make a lower settlement offer, because the plaintiff's attorney appeared unprofessional and unprepared to take the case to trial. The plaintiff's counsel showed his cards by not having the mediation at a neutral location, thus providing the other side with a significant advantage.

Finally, if strong egos are involved, letting the other side gain a perceived face-saving victory by having you negotiate at his office may lead him to give you something to bargain with in return.

The reality is that the location of the negotiation can change the dynamics considerably.

TIMING IS EVERYTHING

Everybody is familiar with the phrase "Timing is everything." This statement is also true for negotiations. The timing of the negotiation is so critical, it can make the difference between a successful resolution and a frustrating waste of time.

Adversaries generally are not prepared to negotiate until either they feel that they need what you're offering or they cannot successfully complete their mission, project, or task without negotiating. If they feel that there is a valid alternative that doesn't require negotiations, they will likely take it.

Several factors affect whether a case is ripe for resolution. One of the key factors is whether a stalemate is painful to both sides. Just as with the 1980s workout slogan "no pain, no gain," each party to a dispute must feel the pain, and the negotiation needs to be the medicine. The "pain" may be simply that they realize they would be better off with a change. Maybe the "pain" is that the parties know they will be more efficient with a deal in place. But there must be some recognition that they can't go on like this.

Another important factor in determining whether the parties are ready to negotiate is whether they both understand their own power as well as the opponent's. In a recent negotiation with Wal-Mart, Spitz International, a supplier of sunflower seeds, sought to get Wal-Mart to pay more money for its products. While Wal-Mart is notoriously aggressive in its negotiations, Spitz realized its own power by recognizing the value and unmatched quality of its product. When Wal-Mart refused to agree to the price increase, Spitz refused to sell any more of its product.

Wal-Mart planned to use hardball tactics and simply get another supplier but soon realized it could not replace Spitz's product—Spitz got the price increase. Wal-Mart initially overestimated its power. When it finally realized both sides' respective power, it was ready to negotiate.

Just as spokesman Orson Welles said on behalf of Paul Masson wines, "We will sell no wine before its time," the same is true for negotiations. You shall enter no negotiation before its time.

NEGOTIATING STYLES

Everybody negotiates in a different way, and your particular style will affect the negotiation environment. This section will focus on negotiating styles, general strategies on negotiations as well as worldviews on negotiation styles.

Negotiating styles are not mutually exclusive. Good negotiators exhibit different styles throughout the process. It is important to realize that negotiating styles can and will change with time and circumstances.

People will often assume that others share their same outlook, so people with a particular negotiating style sometimes assume that others negotiate in the same manner; this is not necessarily true.

To be successful in negotiations, you must understand your style as well as the different styles that you will face when negotiating.

COMPETITIVE STYLE

Competitive negotiators focus on winning, often at all costs, and they use hardball tactics to achieve their goals. The basic premise in competitive negotiations is that there is a winner and a loser. Either you get more of the pie or less of the pie. Both parties cannot win. Sometimes this is referred to as a "zero-sum game."

When thinking about negotiating, many people automatically assume the competitive negotiating style is the way to negotiate. Many litigated cases can take on some aspect of competitive negotiations.

In competitive negotiations, the parties are less (or not at all) concerned about maintaining an ongoing relationship with each other. This is the case in personal-injury lawsuits involving drivers who do not know each other. Neither party cares about the other's feelings or what the other side thinks of them. Moreover, one party is asking the other to pay money, and the other party wants to pay the least amount possible. This can create a zero-sum game negotiation and an environment for competitive negotiations.

Signs that you are dealing with a competitive negotiator
- They make lowball offers.
- They rush the process.
- They focus on their interests.
- They use good-cop/bad-cop techniques.
- They focus on a single issue, such as price.

- They use anger as a tactic.
- They dominate the agenda.
- They make statements such as "So what's in it for me?" or "I don't care if you're offended. I'm offended by your offer."

COOPERATIVE STYLE

Cooperative negotiators are generally the opposite of competitive negotiators. They try to find solutions that focus on a "win-win" concept. They will look towards common gains, they will try to find joint interests and to understand how the other side can benefit from the negotiation.

There is a substantial misperception about the effectiveness of cooperative negotiators. In the media, negotiators are typically portrayed as competitive, and many novice negotiators focus on competitive strategies.

However, research has found that cooperative negotiators are considered excellent and effective negotiators. One study, conducted by Professor Gerald R. Williams, found that 65 percent of the queried negotiators were reported to be cooperative problem solvers. Of the negotiators who were considered "effective," 75 percent were cooperative.

In another study, conducted by Neil Rackham and John Carlisle in England, skilled negotiators used classic competitive strategies only 2.3 times per hour, compared to average negotiators, who used such competitive strategies approximately five times more often.

The reality is that many successful negotiators are cooperative and cooperative negotiators are often very effective.

Signs that you are dealing with a cooperative negotiator

- They are interested in understanding your issues and concerns.
- They rephrase your statements.

- They are less concerned with time.
- They ask a lot of open-ended questions.
- They make comments such as "I understand how you feel," or "Help me understand your feelings."

PRAGMATIC STYLE

Pragmatic negotiators make decisions because they are necessary. Their decisions are based upon information that may be limited but that considers the useful data available at the time.

Pragmatic negotiators usually are not influenced by emotional or enthusiastic presentations. As Detective Joe Friday of the classic TV drama *Dragnet* said, "Just the facts, ma'am."

Pragmatic negotiators are focusing on efficiency and time management. These negotiators are extremely punctual; they're the first to arrive and the first to leave. They do not like their time being wasted, and they're not big on small talk.

They will likely try to get to the bottom line fairly quickly and are frustrated by an excessive focus on emotions. Many times, they'd rather walk away from a deal than take the time to save it.

Signs that you are dealing with a pragmatic negotiator

- They constantly look at their watch.
- They use language that is direct and to the point.
- They look at real-world solutions and situations and don't focus on what could have happened.
- When meeting with them in their office, they may have a staff member see you in.
- They focus on the bottom line.
- They will make statements such as "What is the net conclusion?" or "How will this affect the outcome?" or "Get to the point."

EXTROVERTED STYLE

Extroverted negotiators are generally friendly and outgoing. Unlike pragmatic negotiators, they enjoy social banter and chitchat. They are more willing to enter into agreements based upon the nature of the relationships.

Extroverted negotiators often do not focus on the details but look at the big picture. They prefer a consensus view and will attempt to persuade you of their position in order to achieve consensus.

This type of negotiator often makes gut decisions and needs to feel enthusiastic about the deal. In order to help this person make a decision, you should focus on the experience associated with the deal rather than solely on the facts related to the transaction.

Signs that you are dealing with an extroverted negotiator

- They may meet you in the lobby instead of having a staff member meet you.
- They display pictures of family and friends.
- They talk about relationships.
- They do not take your initial answer as the final word.
- They will keep trying to convince you.
- They display a warm and friendly personality.
- They use phrases such as "I have a good feeling about this one," or "I consider myself a good judge of character," or "How does Jack feel about this offer?"

CONFLICT-AVOIDANCE STYLE

These negotiators like to avoid conflict and want to put together deals with the least amount of disruption to their emotional state. Some of these people avoid conflict to the detriment of themselves and their relationships. Rather than seeing conflict as a way to reconcile differences, they see it as a process that causes pain and disruption.

People who avoid conflict do not trust themselves and fear the fallout from conflict. They would rather maintain the status quo than experience the often chaotic nature of change.

Often, this type of negotiator fears what will happen and how the other side will react if the conflict escalates. They like to be in control of the circumstances and the negotiation and will want it to take place in a controlled or controllable environment or manner.

These people are motivated by the status quo. President Obama's campaign of change would not be hold any appeal for them. Helping these people understand that what they are contemplating is not unique or new helps them in negotiations. They also value the appearance of peaceful relations, even if it's just an appearance.

Signs that you are dealing with a conflict-avoidance negotiator

- They get stressed at the slightest sign of conflict.
- They like to have everything in place, including their personal space.
- They are the last to adapt to new changes in the organization.

- They smile at things that insult them.
- They change the topic when something controversial or uncomfortable is being discussed.
- You may hear from a third person about this negotiator's feelings.
- They will say things like "That's not how we normally do it," or "Why doesn't the existing structure work?" or "What about if we handle this later?"

ANALYTICAL PROBLEM-SOLVING STYLE

Analytical problem solvers need information to be able to make decisions—the more information, the better. These negotiators are likely to make sure that before they make any decision, all the i's are dotted and all the t's are crossed.

Charts, graphs, and statistics are helpful decision-making tools to this type of negotiator.

Analytical problem solvers thrive on problems or conflicts for the opportunity they provide to work towards finding solutions. They do not focus on fault but on solutions; they brainstorm many ideas and often think outside the box to find an answer.

For example, if the question is how to split a pot of money, the problem solver might start by asking, "Is there a way for both sides to get the entire pot?"

Signs that you are dealing with an analytical problem-solving negotiator

- They comprehend data faster than most people.
- They focus on the **solution**, not on who caused the problem.
- They may focus on **tough** love.
- They will easily **concede** their weaknesses and strengths.
- They use mathematical **concepts** to solve problems.
- They are good with **spatial** issues.

- They focus on the big picture and solution.
- They make comments such as "What is our objective in this situation?" or "This problem can be summarized as follows," or "Do we have any more data on this issue?"

AMIABLE, ACCOMMODATING STYLE

Amiable, accommodating negotiators are often warm and outgoing but can also be quiet and good listeners. However, despite their friendly demeanor, they are slow to act and reluctant to take risks.

Amiable accommodators are not motivated by fear but by what is safe. They ask themselves, "What is the safe play in this negotiation environment?"

This type of negotiator works best in a team or committee. They require outside approval to be able to make a decision. They will not rock the boat; if the boat is going in the wrong direction, they will change boats. For example, if an amiable accommodator wants to make a deal with you but others on the team don't, this person will likely side with the others on the team.

To make these negotiators feel safe, you need to establish a rapport and trust well before you offer terms. One of the critical questions to answer in the amiable accommodator's mind is "Why?" You must eliminate all risk from the transaction before the amiable accommodator will consent to it.

Signs that you are dealing with an amiable, accommodating negotiator

- They will listen for a while before chiming in.
- They rely on input from others rather than on their own experience.

- They like to experience things "hands-on."
- They are likely to be the last person on a committee to vote.
- They usually won't be the sole dissenting vote.
- They make comments such as "What does Jim have to say about this?" or "It doesn't matter to me which way we go," or "What do the experts say?"

SENSORY LEARNERS AND LEARNING STYLES

Negotiating styles are affected by how people learn and process information. Different people react differently to different types of information.

Typically, there are three ways that people learn: visual, auditory, and physical or tactile.

Visual learners learn through seeing things. They primarily experience the world through their eyes. Visual learners will use language that's based on vision, such as "I see what you're saying." They will describe events through their visual senses, such as "The concert was spectacular, the lighting was awesome. You were so close you could see the drummer…" These people will need to be shown—with charts, graphs, brochures, videos, etc.—why they should negotiate with you. The majority of people in the United States are visual learners.

Auditory learners are those who learn best through hearing things. They love oral reports or testimony and can communicate without notes, based on what they hear. These people say things like, "I hear what you're saying," or "Are you hearing me?" They can be better convinced by having reasons repeated to them orally, and they themselves may repeat what you say to digest the information. They can be influenced by hearing the same information in different ways.

Physical or tactile learners, also called kinesthetic learners, are those who learn through doing and experiencing things themselves. They are hands-on. If you show them something new, they will have to do it themselves before they can comprehend it. They will often say things like "I feel your pain," or "That left a bad taste in my mouth." In describing things, these people may use descriptions like "You could feel the tension in the air." As negotiators they need to experience the benefits of a negotiated deal. This is why many stores use tasting samples—once the kinesthetic learner experiences a product, he or she will be more likely to buy it.

Each of these learning styles affects how a negotiator processes information to arrive at a satisfactory resolution.

AGE CONSIDERATIONS

Another important factor to consider when evaluating how you and your negotiating partner will interact is the way that different age groups view the same set of facts.

For example, on one end of the spectrum, people born before 1946 are products of the Great Depression and World War II. The Depression made them conservative with money. They often lived with extended families, so family values are important. They were raised with church and duty and a strong sense of honor and responsibility. When negotiating with this age group, it is important to appeal to their sense of fairness and what's right and wrong. It is important to show your work ethic and your loyalty.

On the other hand, Generation Xers (or Gen Xers) are completely different in their worldview. They were born between 1965 and 1980. Many of these people had two working parents—their view of the world may be more pessimistic, having been influenced by the Cold War, nuclear proliferation, and terrorism. This generation is typically very entrepreneurial and not afraid to take risks. Their goal is to use technology to reduce work. When negotiating with this generation, be prepared for their willingness to challenge accepted views to see if something can be done better and faster. They reject the concept of having to pay their dues and are less willing to expend a lot of time socializing.

As an interesting side note, many Gen Xers also comment that they consider the next generation, the Millennials, as even less patient and less willing to spend large amounts of time on "idle" chatter or conversation. Remember, the Millennials are the generation of MySpace, Twitter, Facebook, and text and instant messaging.

Each generation has its own unique communication needs and styles. It is valuable to pay attention to those issues when considering how the negotiation will go.

ARE YOU HINDERING THE PROCESS?

Don't let your ego get in the way of your own success in negotiations. Just because you have one primary negotiating does not justify ignoring the other styles to the detriment of a deal.

A good negotiator taps into different styles as time and circumstances dictate. For example, a cooperative negotiator likes to share information and ideas to achieve a win-win situation. When facing a competitive negotiator in a zero-sum negotiation, a cooperative negotiator is at a disadvantage and has to change styles to adapt to the situation or face losing in a "win-lose" dynamic.

On the other hand, if you are a Gen Xer negotiating with a person born before 1946, you may have to change the way you communicate to achieve your objectives. Gen Xers have to be much more patient when interacting with someone who lived through the Great Depression.

Don't be married to your style. Research has shown that some of the most effective negotiators are the ones who can tap into their cooperative and their competitive instincts during a single negotiation.

WHERE TO START

A common question about negotiations and mediations is whether there is a "secret" to making initial offers or demands. Where do you start? That questions, although seemingly simple, is fraught with complexities that depend on the circumstances of each case, and it is impossible to make a definitive statement or create a single formula for starting a negotiation or making an opening offer.

This next section addresses some of the issues involved in making initial offers and how to effectively make offers to get the best results.

UNDERSTAND YOUR RELATIONSHIP WITH YOUR OPPONENT

Before making your initial offer, consider the type of relationship you have with your opponent. Is this is a one-time transaction, such as a personal-injury litigation? Or is this a relationship that must continue in the future, like a business or family relationship?

The evaluation of this relationship is critical, as the wrong initial move could hamper further discussions, and the opening offer will vary based upon the value of the relationship to you.

For example, if two people wish to be ongoing partners, both sides might be inclined to take a moderate or cooperative initial stance to try to preserve the relationship. Studies have shown that the more familiar with each other parties are, the more they are inclined to start in a more moderate posture and make greater concessions. But if the partnership is terminated and the parties will no longer be dealing with each other, the parties might be more inclined to make a more aggressive or competitive opening move.

THE GREATER YOUR EXPECTATIONS, THE GREATER YOUR CHANCE OF RECOVERY

After you have determined the value of the relationship and obtained sufficient information, it is time to shoot for the stars. Regardless of your style or the nature of the relationship, have strong expectations of success. By asking for the impossible, we obtain the best possible.

Studies have shown that in negotiation as well as social contexts, the higher a person's expectations, the better that person will do. One study had two sets of negotiators, with only one difference between them: the expectation of what was considered a satisfactory result. The group that was given the higher expectation consistently outperformed the other group.

This does not, however, mean that you can make an outrageously high or low offer in a vacuum. The "optimistic" offer must at least be supportable by some presentable evidence or argument. It is not necessary to support your initial position with your best argument, but you need to be able to support it with some argument or evidence. The difference between outrageous and optimistic is that the former cannot be supported and the latter is simply the most optimistic evaluation of the facts.

For example, in an employment case alleging sexual harassment, the defendant may open with an offer in the four- or five-figure range. This position can be supported by the fact that many employment cases are won by the defense or awarded only nominal sums. On the other hand, starting with $100 offer might be deemed outrageous.

This principle of "optimistic" offers or demands is supported by additional social and psychological research that has shown, for example, that people are affected by the concept of "anchoring," i.e., when given a set of numbers, most people will subconsciously adjust their expectations based upon the first numbers they hear. When a researcher presented the same string of numbers, from eight to one, people consistently estimated the sum of the numbers to be greater than when they were shown the same string from one to eight. Thus, "optimistic" initial offers might have the effect of anchoring both sides' expectation to a more moderate number.

The secret to making the best opening offer, which allows the continuation of the negotiation process, is that there is no secret, just good judgment under the circumstances.

NEGOTIATING CHIPS

In the game of poker, the object is to accumulate as many chips as you can, until you either win them all or quit the game. When initiating negotiations, the object is the exact opposite. You want to start out with lots of chips and then get ready to give them away. The negotiating chips are different, or additional, parts of an offer that make up the whole package.

For example, when selling your home, you don't just have the price to negotiate; you might be able to negotiate a lot of other chips, such as a free refrigerator, terms of escrow, timing of payments, move-in date, closing costs, and many more.

These chips need not have significant value to you. What's important is whether they are of value to the other side.

To use a recent professional malpractice case as an example, James wanted a letter of apology as a sign that the other side recognized its inappropriate actions. His opponent, on the other hand, didn't care one way or another about the letter, as long as the financial terms were acceptable. By using the letter as a negotiating chip, they secured a better deal on the financial aspect of the settlement.

Another example involved the sale of my home. I was selling the house without appliances. The buyer, a new homeowner, did not want to spend more money out of an already tight budget on appliances such as washer and dryer. I had planned on taking the washer and dryer that were in the house with me. But since they were about ten years old, I decided I needed a new washer and dryer anyway and agreed to leave the old ones to help close the deal.

These negotiating chips give you flexibility to be able to arrive at the best possible agreement.

DEMONSTRATE YOUR COMPETENCE

Power is perception; perception is power. Demonstrating early in the negotiation that you are competent will go a long way towards ensuring a successful result.

Your own opinion of your competence matters less than your opponent's. For example, you may be the greatest employee in the world, but if your boss doesn't think so, you could still lose your job.

In negotiations, people will make judgments about the opposing side, and they will do so mainly based on their perceptions of the other side's competence. Before going to trial, most lawyers research the opposing counsel to find out about their background, experience in a particular field, and number of times they have gone to trial. All of this will inform their own strategy.

In one case that involved many health care issues and decisions, one of the lawyers was trying to explain his client's position in a joint session between the parties. He started explaining intricate medical issues, but since he didn't fully grasp their complex nature, he repeatedly misspoke about the names of conditions, the meaning of lab results, and diagnoses. Later, when I met with the other side privately, the attorney's comments to me were, "Mr. Smith doesn't know the medicine. I know the medicine of this case. If we go to trial, I am going to have an advantage." If you're dealing with an area with which you are not completely familiar, it is better to say as little as possible.

Your competence in your field is an important source of power in your negotiation. Maximize that power.

THE LESS YOU KNOW ABOUT THE OTHER SIDE, THE MORE OPTIMISTIC YOUR INITIAL POSITION SHOULD BE

In the United States, negotiators tend to make their initial positions higher and then work towards their actual goal. Part of the reason is that the negotiators often know very little about the other side. There is no established trust that the other side will be fair in the negotiation, and therein lies the need to start high.

Take a hypothetical house sale. What if I told you that I have a house for you to buy? How much would you offer me? Since you don't know anything about the house—is it a doll house, a dog house, a house in Beverly Hills, or a shack in major need of repair?—your offer should be very low to protect yourself from the risk of a bad deal.

But if I show you a standard property listing with a picture and description of the house and ask you to buy the house, you might be less wary. You still might, however, make a low initial offer because you don't know the condition of the house, the character of the neighborhood and many other important factors.

Only after you have fully inspected the house, looked at the neighborhood, and evaluated every other aspect of the house will you be willing to make your best offer.

The same is true in litigation. Most attorneys will either make very high or very low opening settlement proposals, depending on which side they represent, since they know little about the other side and whether all the representations from that side are true. As they learn more, they are more willing to make a more reasonable offer.

Information is the key to helping you develop trust. The more you trust your negotiating partner, the more reasonable your demand is likely to be. Note that the opposite holds true also, (the less you know, the less you can trust) which can limit your negotiation options from the beginning.

ESTABLISH A FRIENDLY RAPPORT WITH YOUR OPPONENT EARLY

There is an old saying that you catch more flies with honey than with vinegar, meaning you will accomplish more, and get more people to help you, by being kind and friendly rather than mean and hurtful. Researchers have found that negotiators get better results by building rapport and connections with their opponents.

People will do things for and react favorably to people they like—that is common sense. There is no right or wrong way of trying to establish a rapport with your opponent. Even if you make a mistake, shake it off and try again.

In the movie *Basic*, John Travolta, as a DEA agent, tries to interrogate a suspect about a possible murder. He tries to develop a rapport by asking the suspect whether he had a favorite baseball team. The suspect answers that he doesn't like baseball. Travolta instantly changes tactics by asking why he doesn't like baseball. No matter the topic, Travolta got the suspect talking, which established a rapport between them that finally paid off when the suspect admitted to killing the victim.

There are several ways that you can establish a rapport with someone. Do something nice for the person. Giving a gift or doing a favor for someone can create goodwill and rapport.

As discussed earlier, researchers have discovered that gift giving invokes the principle of reciprocity, which refers to the fact that people feel obligated to return a received favor.

Another way to establish a connection with another person is to identify and build on similarities between the two of you. Studies have found that people who have gone through the same experiences have closer bonds. The more similar you are, the more likely you are to build a relationship.

Imagine how you react to someone who is from your hometown or who went to the same high school as you. You and that person have something in common. Now imagine your first meeting with a person who went to your high school, comes from your hometown, has many of the same friends as you, and likes the same types of movies and music. Do you think you might be prone to liking that person from the very beginning? I sure would.

ESTABLISH INITIAL COMMITMENTS

Before you negotiate the terms of a transaction or deal, you will often need to establish certain commitments as to how the negotiation will proceed.

In the 2008 presidential election, this became an issue. Senator McCain criticized then-Senator Obama for stating that he would sit down with countries such as Iran without preconditions. In other words, McCain was criticizing Obama for his willingness to enter into diplomatic negotiations without first obtaining certain fundamental commitments.

In many mediations, the parties may need to establish certain parameters to the negotiations. For example, in one case, an attorney for an insurance company insisted that the only way he would even entertain discussions was if the plaintiff was willing to consider an amount within the insurance policy limit. Otherwise, negotiations could not take place. In another case, one side requested that the other side commit to bringing the top people from the company to the mediation as a precondition to entering negotiations.

Sometimes the parties need to commit to establishing certain ground rules. For example, one party might say, "Can we agree that we need to arrive at a fair price for your product?" Or it might be a question of a procedural commitment, such as "Can we agree that we will address the issue of employee salary before we address any issues of benefits and length of employment?"

Early commitments can also act as a foundation for larger commitments. Each commitment adds to the parties' ability to foster trust and build consensus. Once smaller agreements are made, it is easier to agree on the larger issues, because the parties have a basis to work from and feel more comfortable with each other.

PEOPLE VALUE THINGS LESS IF THEY COME FROM THE OTHER SIDE

Sometimes negotiations seem dysfunctional, for example when one side makes concessions that the other side perceives as insignificant simply because it is the adversary who offered the concession. This tendency is called "reactive devaluation."

There are several reasons for this phenomenon, the main one being a lack of trust between the parties—the concession is likely to be viewed negatively because it was offered by someone who cannot be fully trusted.

To avoid this phenomenon, negotiators must take steps to establish trust and rapport as well as investigate the needs of the other side. By doing so, they will discover their opponent's motivations and will make offers the other side can accept.

Another way to combat reactive devaluation is to make the other side believe the concession was their idea in the first place. Sir Winston Churchill did just that when he sought to convince the United States to invade North Africa during World War II. The American military commanders saw no benefit in invading North Africa, but Churchill made Roosevelt feel as if the idea was his own—from which point on Roosevelt supported the idea wholeheartedly, despite his military advisors' recommendations against it.

DON'T MAKE AN OFFER UNTIL YOU ARE READY

Sometimes people make the big mistake of making an offer when they are not ready to do so. This premature offer can create multiple problems.

First, it might not be the right offer. It could be based on a lack of information or understanding of the true nature of the situation. This was true for the Beatles, when they were negotiating the price for their appearance in the movie *A Hard Day's Night*. At the time, the Beatles' manager, Brian Epstein, had no experience in the movie industry. The studios pressured him to give them a price. In a meeting with the movie's producer, Epstein stated that he wouldn't accept less than 7½ percent of the income from the movie. The problem was that Epstein didn't know what the market was for such a commodity—as it turned out, United Artists, the studio that financed the film, had a figure of 25 percent as a starting point for the negotiations! Epstein's offer was a critical negotiating error, because he jumped in too soon.

If you aren't ready to make an offer, don't let yourself get pressured into it. Do your homework first, and then consider making your offer once you're fully prepared.

WHO HAS THE AUTHORITY TO NEGOTIATE?

Many people have started negotiations, only to find out that the person they were negotiating with had no authority to make a decision. Not only does that make the interaction a waste of time, it could create opportunities for a competitive negotiator on the other side to take advantage of you.

For example, in one case involving a real estate transaction, two sets of husbands and wives were arguing over a house that had been sold with many structural and cosmetic defects. In an attempt to resolve their dispute, the sellers made an offer to the other husband (the buyer). He responded with his own offer, which the sellers considered acceptable.

But when the sellers went to finalize the deal in writing, the wife, who also was a necessary party to the purchase, announced that her husband wasn't authorized to speak for them and that his offer was not acceptable to her. The parties did not have a deal at that moment and had to continue negotiations until the wife was satisfied with the terms. Because the sellers had not made sure to negotiate with the proper person, they ended up losing time and money in the end.

The moral of the story: Always make sure you're talking with the person who has the authority to finalize the agreement.

CONSIDER YOUR PROPOSAL FROM YOUR OPPONENT'S PERSPECTIVE

How will the other side perceive your offer? Many people forget to ask this question before making their initial offer, only to be surprised when the other party reacts in a manner that they did not expect.

This was a lesson I learned long ago when making an offer to purchase a home. At the time, the country was going through a recession and the housing market was a buyer's market; the prices were lower than they had been in years. My wife and I had found a house we liked, and given the tough market for sellers, we thought that even if we made an offer the seller didn't like, he would still counter-offer with an amount that was lower than the stated price. In fact, we fully expected the seller to counter. So we made an offer to purchase the house for far less than the list price. The response was crickets—nothing.

When I inquired of our agent why the seller had not countered, she responded that the seller was insulted and would not even entertain such an offer. She explained that the seller had bought the house several years earlier, when the market was high, and had just recently reduced the price significantly. With his mortgage likely close to the amount of his asking price, the seller probably had a very small profit margin. In short, the agent said, given our extremely low offer, why should the seller even bother?

That question made me realize the importance of understanding how the other side will perceive an offer before I make it.

ACKNOWLEDGE THE OTHER PERSON'S PROBLEMS BEFORE ASKING THEM TO HELP YOU

Stephen Covey, in his book *The 7 Habits of Highly Effective People*, identifies seven traits or skills that he believes will make a person effective in all aspects of life. Habit number 5 is "Seek First to Understand, Then to Be Understood: Principles of Mutual Understanding." This principle, although not specifically a negotiating strategy, is directly relevant to negotiators.

If you're asking a person to consider an offer that you have made, you should make sure to understand why that person should be speaking with you in the first place. Consider the offer from her perspective and, more importantly, acknowledge your counterpart's concerns and issues. If you show her that you understand her concerns, she will be more willing to entertain *your* concerns and proposals. If you don't acknowledge her concerns, why should she acknowledge yours?

In one very emotional negotiation involving the death of a woman at a health care facility, the owner of the facility was about to convey her last, best and final offer to the family of the deceased—an offer that was far below what the family was asking. The owner, however, explained to the family that she understood their feelings; she, too, had suffered the loss of a loved one and knew how it felt. She explained that she understood why the family might be angry at the circumstances of the loss and expressed her desire to listen to any other concerns the family had so that she might fully understand their situation.

After the family had described their concerns, the owner described her own problems that came with operating a health care facility. She explained that she was going to make her final offer, which was all she could afford to pay, given the company's budgetary problems, and that additional payments would bankrupt her. She also promised to institute changes—based on the family's concerns—aimed at preventing any such future occurrences.

After long consideration, the family accepted the offer and told the owner that they appreciated her willingness to hear their concerns and her pledge to work hard to make changes. That agreement would never have happened if the owner had not first sought to understand, and then to be understood.

LET THE OTHER SIDE UNDERESTIMATE YOUR SKILLS

In his book *The Art of War,* the Chinese philosopher Sun Tzu wrote, "He who exercises no forethought but makes light of his opponents is sure to be captured by them." In other words, never underestimate your opponent, neither in negotiations nor in life.

On the other hand, you should certainly try to let the other side underestimate you. That doesn't mean that you demonstrate incompetence. Instead, it means that you shouldn't show all your cards. Hold something back in case you need to use it later.

The other reason to let people feel that you are not as good, smart, or intelligent as they are is because it disarms them. Most people will be insulted if you attack their intelligence. In fact, many people go to great lengths to justify the successes of others: "Well, he had an Ivy League education," or "Her family has money." By letting the other person feel superior in some way, you will not only disarm them but potentially make them your ally because they aren't threatened by you.

In 1865, the Prussian leader Otto Von Bismarck wanted the Austrians to sign a treaty protecting Prussia. The Austrian leader liked to play cards and professed to being able to judge a person's character by the way they played cards. Bismarck proceeded to play cards in the most dismal manner. He made mistakes, revealed his strategy, and lost a lot of money. He made aggressive moves and appeared to not think ahead. When the time came to sign the treaty, the Austrian leader believed that Bismarck could not possibly have the mental agility to draft a strategic treaty that could damage

Austria, so he signed it. Bismarck got what he wanted!

In negotiations, it never pays to reveal your true intelligence or your true position. It's better to let the other side underestimate your skills.

FOCUS ON THE FEW GOOD POINTS

Ludwig Mies van der Rohe, the architect of minimalist design, famously said that "less is more," in other words, you don't need a lot of bells and whistles to sell your look or product. In selling your offer or proposal, you don't need 1,001 reasons; you just need one good reason to convince the other side to accept your view.

The key to limiting yourself to a few key points or arguments is to make sure that you don't sound like you are repeating yourself. Change the way you deliver your message. When you add additional points or issues, you simply give the other side an opportunity to attack your weaker arguments.

I learned this the hard way in trial when I was a young lawyer. In a medical malpractice case, I presented three theories why the health care provider's actions were inappropriate. My first argument was strong and irrefutable—I even had pictures to prove it! The other arguments were not as strong. Opposing counsel, knowing how to capitalize on even the smallest weakness, attacked my third argument and found a way for the jury to question whether it was correct or not. Then he then said something I won't ever forget. "Ladies and gentlemen of the jury, I have shown you that Mr. Mehta's third theory probably doesn't make sense. If you don't agree with Mr. Mehta's third argument, then what is to say that you can agree with his first argument?"

He put doubt in the jury's mind regarding my strongest argument. He reminded them that I had presented three arguments and that I believed in all of them. Therefore, if I was wrong on one of them, then I certainly could be wrong on all three of them.

That attorney took my indisputable case and made it look weak. Eventually, the divided jury agreed with him—they had some doubts!

Be careful what arguments you present to support your offer.

ASK THE OTHER SIDE TO COMMIT TO SOMETHING YOU KNOW IS WRONG (AND CAN BE PROVEN WRONG)

Sometimes, it is helpful to see if the other side will commit to something that you know is wrong. This strategy is designed to make the other side doubt their position. In trial, the golden rule of cross-examination is to never ask a question to which you don't already know the answer.

In negotiations, the point is not that you shouldn't ask questions but to make sure that you know the answer to the question before you ask it. If the other side answers the question wrong, you gain a piece of ammunition to show why your offer or position is better; in other words, the other side's perception of your "power" increases.

For example, in a recent negotiation involving a maintenance contract, the owner of a computer company claimed that his price was the best deal for people buying service contracts for computers. He tried to make it appear that the customers were getting a good deal by accepting his service contract. The customer, however, had done his research and found that other companies provided similar services for less. The interaction went like this:

Customer: "I am sure that you understand that one of my concerns is to get the best price for my service contract because of financial limitations."

Owner:	"Yes, I can understand that. That is why our prices are fair. We offer very reasonable prices."
Customer:	"I want to just understand what you are saying about your prices. All in, with all expenses, is your service contract the lowest price out there? And I have your word on that?"
Owner:	"Yes, you have my word."
Customer:	"O.K. Great! My concern is that we would like to be with your company, but we have researched the other companies in the neighborhood, and their prices are in fact lower than your price."

The customer then showed him the other companies' prices and asked if he would match their lower price. The owner, faced with losing face in front of the customer or, worse, appearing dishonest, was forced to accept the lower price.

Knowing the answer to the question before you ask it can be invaluable during negotiations.

THE NEGOTIATION

Negotiation tactics and strategies are often varied and should adapt to the situation. Typically, you cannot conduct a negotiation with a limited arsenal of strategies and tactics.

One of the key ingredients to a successful negotiation is creativity. The more creative you are in coming up with solutions, the better.

This section is designed to give you a new outlook on negotiating strategies. Not all of the strategies will apply to your circumstances. Some of them will be more applicable in a competitive negotiation environment, while others will work better in a cooperative environment. Some of the strategies will provide you with tools to manage the negotiation.

It is helpful to consider the negotiation strategies and tactics, as well as the other tips in this book, as tools in a toolbox. When you come to a negotiation, you want to make sure you have all the tools in your toolbox. You may decide that the situation requires a hammer, or maybe it requires a wrench; and on some occasions, you might need multiple tools to take care of the situation.

This section is designed to fill your toolbox. Some of the chapters discuss specialty tools, others everyday tools. Every toolbox should have a good mix of both.

RANGE BARGAINING

Sometimes the parties cannot agree on the exact price or terms. They may need to discuss ranges, so that they can agree on the arena or framework within which they are willing to negotiate.

Many lawyers talk about the ranges as "ballparks." Sometimes the parties start out in two different ballparks or try to test the waters by finding out if they are even in the same ballpark.

If you are negotiating a buyout of a partner's share of a business, each partner may have a very different view of the value of the business and, therefore, the value of each partner's share. One partner might suggest that he would be willing to entertain discussions within the range of $1 million to $2 million. By providing the range, the partner has indicated a willingness to be somewhat flexible. At the same time, he has not stated exactly what he would be willing to pay - $1 million, $1,5 million, $2 million, or some other number.

This tactic works well when a substantial amount of information, but no exact information, is known about the item being negotiated. In the partnership situation the partners may not know the exact gross sales, the prior year's tax picture, the exact nature of liabilities, or the obligations of the business.

Rather, the range allows the parties to understand that there are certain parameters to the negotiation, but that the parameters are not unlimited.

WHAT IF...

What if I were to get the price down to $100, would you be willing to buy that product from me?

This strategy often works well when you have limited negotiating power and don't have authority to make a proposal. "What if...?" allows you to continue negotiating and to create an environment of hope.

This strategy also gives you a way out if you cannot get the price you really want. For example, if you get the client committed to a "what if" price of, say, $100, but your boss or supervisor wanted you to close at $105, you might then say, "I tried to get the price down to $100, but he just won't do it. He did say he'd do it for $105." Given the fact that the client was already committed to $100, the new price of $105 is reasonably close.

The "what if" technique can also be used to ask the other side what would happen if they didn't enter into a deal with you. This kind of question allows you to show the other side their alternatives, and hopefully those alternatives are not as good as making a deal with you.

HOW MUCH? OR, YOU WANT *WHAT*??

Many times people will have a knee-jerk response to an unexpected situation. You might hear them say things like, "You have got to be kidding me," or "I can't believe you just did that." These types of reactions can be used in negotiations.

When your opponent makes an offer, especially if you deem the offer to be unreasonably low, you can respond with a knee-jerk "You want it for *how much*?" This response is usually accompanied by an incredulous look or attitude. You want the other side to second-guess their offer.

In response to your over-the-top reaction, the other side may inadvertently reveal information about their offer. In one case, involving a personal-injury claim, the plaintiff made a demand that he believed was reasonable under the circumstances. The defendants responded by demonstrating shock that the plaintiff would start out so high. The defendants asked me, as the mediator, to confirm with the plaintiff that the initial offer was not a typographical error, because they were sure that such an offer could not reasonably be made if the plaintiff really wanted to settle the case.

The plaintiff confidentially told me that he knew his number was high and that he didn't expect the defendants to get even close to that number but he didn't know how the defendants would react.

Later, after the mediation was over, the defendants revealed that they thought the plaintiff's initial number was reasonable as a starting position, but that they just wanted to lower his expectations of the end result. The tactic worked—the plaintiff second-guessed himself and came back with a lower number.

Smart negotiators recognize this gambit for what it is. They respond that they believe their price to be reasonable but that they are open to hearing why the other side would consider it outrageous. By doing so, they can now elicit information regarding the ultimate position of the side who feigned outrage.

MAKE TWO OFFERS

Sometimes you can make two offers to your opponent, each one emphasizing a different thing. Usually, you can make such an offer if you either know or are trying to find out what motivates the other side. Multiple offers often work during negotiations involving multiple issues.

The following illustrates how this might work.

Joe sells heavy medical equipment. A medical office is interested in purchasing his products. Joe understands that many companies might be concerned about the necessary initial capital outlay. So Joe may make the following offers.

The sale price is $100,000 for the equipment. This can be financed over a period of five years. If the buyer wants to obtain his own financing, however, Joe would offer a 10-percent discount.

In many litigation cases there is a need for future payments to protect an income stream or to pay for medical expenses. The parties may negotiate one term for a straight cash payment and a different amount for a payment stream, also known as a structured settlement, over a period of time.

For example, an insurance company might offer to pay a one-time sum of $100,000 now, or pay $20,000 now and $1,000 a month for the rest of the person's life.

By making multiple offers, you can create a compromise that suits both parties.

YOU'LL HAVE TO DO BETTER THAN THAT

Sometimes, you can tell the other side that they will have to do better than what they have offered. To use this technique, you simply respond to an offer by stating, "You'll have to do better than that." In essence, you are telling the other side that their proposal doesn't even tempt you. This technique is slightly different from the "You Want What" technique in that you have made a specific counter outright rejecting your opponent's offer in this technique, where you may still have the option to accept some part of the offer in the "You want What" technique.

This technique is best used when there is a lot of uncertainty as to the price of the commodity or the product being negotiated.

A downside of this approach is that you have drawn a line in the sand; you have indicated that you won't negotiate unless the other side provides you with a better offer.

Lawyers often try to use this technique, and sometimes it even works. However, sophisticated negotiators will respond that the offer they have made still stands and that they are here to negotiate but will not bid against themselves. They will state that if the other side doesn't like the offer, they should make their own proposal.

Another risk associated with this technique is that you might alienate the other side early in the negotiation. As this approach does not lend itself to building a rapport, it should be used sparingly.

DON'T FOCUS ON YOUR BOTTOM LINE

How many times have you heard someone referring to the bottom line? Or perhaps you have heard the question, "What's the bottom line?" Our society's general fascination with the bottom line affects the way negotiations take place.

It is important to understand that the bottom line, although important, should not be the focus of negotiations. In fact, obsessing over the bottom line of a negotiation is a major mistake that could cost you considerably. The three main problems with focusing on the bottom line are burning out too fast, revealing your true intentions, and causing other people to focus on your bottom line as well.

First, when people focus on the bottom line in negotiations, they burn out, or peak too soon—they expend all their energy getting to one specific point, leaving no mental or emotional energy after that point has been reached. Once that principal objective is reached, they no longer negotiate with the same vigor that they had when they were trying to reach the objective.

As an example, if a person was told that he or she must run 100 yards as fast as possible, once the person has crossed the "finish line," she visibly loses energy and immediately slows down. If an outsider, however, didn't know how far the runner had to go, it would become clear once the runner loses energy. In negotiations, your opponent won't know how far you are supposed to go unless you reveal it by your actions. This principle is also based on basic survival instinct. The caveman hunter could only rest after he caught his prey. Up until that time, he must remain vigilant.

In negotiations, the classic example of "peaking too soon" is in the automobile purchasing process. Invariably, the car salesperson wears the buyer down to find out what the buyer's highest price will be to purchase the car. After the negotiation for the car is completed, the buyer gets this feeling of relief, as if she finally achieved her goal of getting the car at the right price. Her mental and emotional energy has been spent.

However, the negotiations have only begun. The salesperson then offers small options such as a security package, a window tinting package, the under-coating package, a service package, and a long-term financing program. Research has proven that there is a greater likelihood of selling small extras after the large purchase has been negotiated. After all, if you have negotiated a $25,000 deal, what is an extra $500 for tinted windows? These small items are where the dealership can really make its money.

Also, when people are too focused on one thing, they may inadvertently give clear signs showing the object of their focus. For example, when people mean to say one thing but are really focusing on another, they sometimes make a Freudian slip that will reveal their true focus. The classic movie example is when a character is focusing on a person's anatomy and then inadvertently mentions that anatomy in conversation.

The same thing occurs in a negotiation. If a person is too focused on the bottom line, she will tend to give that bottom line away by her actions. Sometimes it will be a slip of the tongue revealing the object of the focus; and other times it is a statement such as "You haven't even gotten to a $100,000, and I can't seriously negotiate with you until then." Regardless of the statement, an astute negotiator will listen to those clues and probe to find out if that slip-up or statement truly is a bottom line.

The third problem with focusing on the bottom line is that others will also focus on it. Unconsciously, once someone else knows your bottom line, they will focus on trying to get to that number. It is human nature to go the path of least resistance.

Instead of focusing on the bottom line, the sophisticated negotiator will focus on the goals that he or she wants to achieve. Although one should always be aware of the bottom line, the true focus should not be on what must happen for the deal to take place but what you would like the deal to look like.

For example, someone enters a negotiation knowing that the maximum he is willing to pay is $100,000 but aiming for $50,000. During the course of the negotiations, he will focus on the $50,000 and will target the negotiations to that amount. If it becomes apparent that the goal is not achievable, he can always reassess and adjust that goal.

Your goal in every negotiation should not be to focus on the bottom line. Instead, focus on creating realistic but optimistic expectations. By doing so, you will not only negotiate better, you will ultimately increase your bottom line.

MAINTAIN LIMITED AUTHORITY

The ability to maintain limited authority in a negotiation is an extremely powerful negotiating tactic. This tactic essentially gives you the flexibility to reevaluate the deals that you negotiate after having thought about the proposal. In essence, the negotiator with limited authority tells the other side he or she must run any potential deals by an unseen higher authority. Sometimes, this higher authority exists, but other times the higher authority is just a fiction that the negotiator has created to gain an edge.

There is always a way to create an appearance of limited authority. Usually, you want to wait to reveal that you have only limited authority. For example, if you are buying a car, you can claim that you have to get approval of the final deal from your spouse. If you are negotiating the sale of a business, you may say that you have to get your partner's approval. Even if you are single, not in a partnership, and don't have any meaningful commitments, you can still say that you have to get the approval of your business advisor.

Imagine, on the other hand, if you state that you have complete authority to finalize all aspects of the deal. What if the other side pushes you into a corner? Do you say, "I just don't want to do the deal you propose"? Wouldn't you rather be able to say, "That sounds like an interesting proposal, but I am going to have to get the approval of the other managers before I can make a decision"?

On the other hand, if you want to avoid being on the receiving end of that tactic, ask to make sure that all the decision makers are present right from the start. That is why, when you go to a timeshare sales seminar, they always ask that you *and* your spouse attend.

If the tactic still is used on you, you can ask the person you are negotiating with to agree with you on the deal points. Then you can ask that person to "sell it" it to the people with the ultimate authority, and ask him whether he will recommend it. Getting that person to commit will help flush out whether he is bluffing or not.

Finally, you can ask to speak with the higher authority yourself. This not only allows you to get to the source, but it also determines whether that higher authority exists in the first place.

LISTEN WITH A GOAL IN MIND

There is an ancient Chinese proverb that says, "To listen well is as powerful a means of influence as to talk well, and is as essential to all true conversation." In negotiations, the more information you have, the more options and tools that you have. And the only way you will get that information is by listening.

Listening does not just mean that you are awake and use your ears. It means you listen actively and with a purpose—to understand the other side. You must listen with your ears, eyes, and body. In other words, you must physically hear what the other person says, you must look at them to see what they say, and you must face them and be open to what they say.

Your attitude must be "I am here to listen and understand."

The ability to truly listen is a gift. According to Brenda Ueland, an author: "Listening is a magnetic and strange thing, a creative force. The friends who listen to us are the ones we move towards. When we are listened to, it creates us, makes us unfold and expand." People appreciate that you listen, and they will return the favor and listen when you need to be heard.

Authors Lesikar and Flatley have proposed the Ten Commandments of Listening. These rules are important to successful negotiations:

1. STOP TALKING! You cannot listen if you are talking.
2. PUT THE SPEAKER AT EASE. Help her feel that she is free to talk.

3. SHOW THAT YOU WANT TO LISTEN. Listen to understand, rather than to oppose.
4. REMOVE DISTRACTIONS.
5. EMPATHIZE. Put yourself in the other person's place to see her point of view.
6. BE PATIENT. Allow plenty of time. Don't interrupt.
7. HOLD YOUR TEMPER.
8. AVOID ARGUMENTS AND CRITICISM. Otherwise, even if you win, you will lose.
9. ASK QUESTIONS. This is encouraging, shows you are listening, and increases your understanding of the issues.
10. STOP TALKING! This is first and last, because all the other commandments depend on it. You simply cannot be a good listener while you are talking.

These commandments of listening make clear that there is a difference between simply hearing someone and truly listening. Oftentimes the difference between a successful and a frustrating negotiation is the ability to be heard.

BE SILENT

The principal rule of listening is to be silent. Silence at the right time can be one of the most powerful and influential negotiating tools. It can be used in almost any situation—when you are given an offer that is overwhelmingly great, when someone asks you a question you don't want to answer, or when you are faced with a tough situation.

Most people feel uncomfortable with silence and want to fill the void by saying something—a fact you can use to your advantage. Silence is deadly because the other person doesn't know what you are thinking and begins to wonder: Are you thinking this is good or bad? Are you going to leave or stay? This lack of knowledge can create a lack of control, and people hate not being in control of a situation.

Silence also buys you time to think. In litigation, lawyers will train witnesses to wait a second or two before answering a question. That time allows them to collect their thoughts. The same is true in negotiations.

Moreover, when you are silent, you are open to watching or listening to what is going on around you. You can take in the situation and gain more knowledge, which, in turn, will better equip you to negotiate.

Finally, when you limit what you say, it is very hard for the other side to use your statements against you. Louis XIV used this to his advantage. In his later years, he was known to be very sparse with his words. No one knew what he was thinking, so everyone was on edge and worried that they would say something that would displease him.

Silence is golden for many reasons.

BE PATIENT

Rome wasn't built in a day and neither are negotiations. Be patient with the process. As sports agent Leigh Steinberg once said, effective negotiators require "tremendous patience and persistence, as well as physical stamina, resilience, and perseverance."

Time and time again, I have been in negotiations where patience has paid off. I often tell parties and their attorneys whose cases I mediate, "The side with the most patience will often get the best deal."

In one case, I was an attorney negotiating on behalf of a wonderful family that had been in a terrible car accident, in which several of the members of the family sustained severe injuries that required multiple surgeries because the right passenger wheel had fallen off while driving. We entered into serious negotiations with the car dealership whom we believed had improperly repaired the vehicle to compensate the family for their suffering and loss.

During the negotiations, the other side offered a sizable number. The family was stressed because they wanted to be finished with the negotiations and move on with their lives. But I was confident that there was some wiggle room and encouraged the family to have patience and to counter with a number that was higher than the last offer but not so high that the other side would simply walk.

Two weeks later, the other side asked if my clients would be willing to split the difference between the two amounts. My clients were willing, and they benefited significantly from a little patience.

In the famous words of Benjamin Franklin, "He that can have patience can have what he will."

GOOD COP/BAD COP

Almost every police drama you have ever seen has a good-cop/bad-cop scene. This strategy involves two negotiators; one plays the bad cop who browbeats the opponent and makes him feel miserable. When the victim feels defeated, the good cop befriends the victim and lets him know that he will try to protect him from the "bad cop." This tactic can lead to substantial disclosures. One of the funniest good-cop/bad-cop scenes was in the *Pink Panther* remake, where Inspector Clouseau, played by Steve Martin, plays both the good cop and the bad cop.

Regardless of how much the tactic has been dramatized and parodied, it still seems to work and continues to be used in numerous negotiations. In car sales, the car salesperson may befriend the potential buyer, while the sales manager will play hardball with the price. The salesperson will act reasonable and appear to act on behalf of the buyer—all with the purpose of closing the deal and score one for the dealership.

Many times in legal negotiations, the lawyer plays the role of the good cop. She might say to the opposing party, "I think your offer is reasonable. If it were up to me, I would accept it in a heartbeat. But I am not in charge. I have to do what my client says, and he simply won't accept those terms." The lawyer acts as the good cop and depicts the client as the bad cop.

There are numerous ways this strategy can be used. In the movie *Basic* as discussed previously, John Travolta, playing a DEA agent interrogating a murder suspect, tells his partner in the investigation, played by Connie Nielsen, to play the bad cop at a certain point. When that time comes, Nielsen threatens to send the suspect to jail for the rest of his life.

In a surprising turn Travolta tells the suspect that Nielsen's actions were "what is known as the good-cop/bad-cop technique," but that he won't play that game. By revealing the technique for what it is and claiming to want no part of it, Travolta, in reality, plays a superb game of good cop/bad cop and ends up as the good cop.

NEGOTIATE TO THE OTHER SIDE'S NEEDS, NOT TO YOURS

Many people feel that simply because they want something, there is no reason that the other side shouldn't give it. In other words, people make the mistake of making offers that they consider reasonable based on their own needs instead of the needs of the other side.

It is well accepted that everybody is motivated by something. The trick is to find out what that something is. A guiding principle of motivation is that people do things for *their* reasons, not for yours.

An example of not considering the other side's motivation was in the movie *Jerry Maguire*. Jerry is a sports agent who has lost all his superstar clients and is left with one client, Rod Tidwell, an Arizona Cardinals wide receiver who does not have a contract and is a relative unknown in the National Football League. Jerry really needs a contract for Rod so that he can get a commission and regain his status as a star agent.

During training, Jerry tells the Cardinals coach that they need to renegotiate Tidwell's contract. The two are scheduled to meet, but the coach stands Jerry up. When Jerry calls to find out what happened, the coach replies that Tidwell doesn't listen, that he has attitude. The coach says he wants the "prototypical wide receiver" who does not complain in the locker room. Jerry reminds the coach that he introduced him to his wife and that they have history together—and then asks the coach to do him a favor and give Tidwell a contract. The coach reminds Jerry that he is no longer a super agent with superstar clients and superstar clout and says, "Jerry, now it's your turn to stand at the back of the line."

Jerry failed to recognize that the deal he really wanted simply was not in the coach's interest. The coach wanted a smart ball player and was not about to pay millions of dollars simply because Jerry wanted it or because Jerry and he had "history together."

When negotiating, look at the other side's motivation and tailor your offer to meet those needs. By doing so, you will eventually satisfy your need to arrive at a deal.

THE (LIMITED) POWER OF NORMS

A norm is defined as a model or pattern that's considered standard. For example, the norm for married couples in the U.S. is to have 2.3 kids—although I must admit that I have never met a couple with 2.3 children. The norm can be a powerful tool in negotiations to demonstrate that your proposal is standard or acceptable. But remember, the existence of a norm does not mean that all people will agree to it.

When negotiating, you can try to use norms or comparable data as a basis to guide the other person in your direction. This principle is applied daily in the real estate market—before people buy or sell a house, they want to know the "comps," or the comparable sales for similar houses.

However, every house is unique, and the comps only set the guidelines. They are not the be-all and end-all for determining a price. You may consider many other things. In fact, if someone tries to use the "norms" technique against you, your response could be that there are many unique things about your specific situation that take it out of the realm of the norms.

PEOPLE DEFER TO AUTHORITY

It's common knowledge that people will generally defer to authority. However, most people don't realize just how powerful authority can be in influencing people's decisions.

For example, studies have consistently shown that the mere fact that a perceived authority figure approves it is enough for an average person to commit the equivalent of torture in many or most cultures.

In the famous Milgram study, the researchers told participants who played the role of "teacher" to deliver continued and progressively more painful electric shocks to other participants, who played the role of "students," when they answered questions incorrectly. Simply because the researchers were in a position of authority, the typical "teacher" was willing to dole out dangerous and potentially fatal electric shocks. Furthermore, most of the "teachers" did not quit their job even when the "students" pleaded, begged, screamed, or agonizingly shouted for the "teacher" to stop.

Why would seemingly normal people do such a depraved thing? Milgram explained that people have a deep-seated inability to defy the wishes of someone in authority, such as a boss or a lab-coated researcher. Subsequent studies have proven Milgram right, and some research has found that even just a slight appearance of authority can create similar responses. Things such as title, clothing, or position can have an "authority" effect. For example, one study, conducted in the Midwest, found that 95 percent of nurses, when given a clearly invalid order to administer double the maximum allowable dose of a drug to a patient, were willing to comply simply because someone who claimed to be a doctor told them to.

Try to find ways to project authority in order to enhance your ability to negotiate. Many of these ways will be very subtle. For example, prominently display any awards you have earned that attest your competence. Wear clothing that demonstrates power. There is a reason they call it a power suit.

When facing an opponent, you should also carefully evaluate whether they in turn are using subtle symbols of authority to influence you, such as claiming, "The president of the corporation authorized me to make this offer."

People defer to authority figures. Make sure you are one.

IF IT'S IMPORTANT ENOUGH TO DO, DO IT IN PERSON

In today's environment more and more things are being accomplished at a distance. Numerous technologies allow us to conduct business from great distances: the phone, the fax, the cell phone, email, text messaging, virtual meetings, web meetings, and the list goes on. But no matter how much the technology advances, there is no substitute for meeting in person.

In the movie *We Are Marshall*, which is based on a true story, Marshall College has been devastated by an airplane crash that cost the lives of almost the entire varsity football team. The college sought to rebuild their program at a late stage in the football season. At the time, the football rules prohibited freshmen from playing on the teams. Marshall was able to recruit only freshmen, because the other schools had already recruited the top players, and without a rule change Marshall was going to be severely hampered in its ability to play football.

The president of the school had made numerous requests to the league to change or waive the rule—without success. He then sat down with the coach to tell him of the many letters he had written on their behalf, when the coach asked him whether he had proposed to his wife in writing. The president, of course, said no, but the question made him realize that he needed to ask the league in person. He did, and the team got its waiver.

If the negotiation is important, it is always better to go in person to try to negotiate the deal or the terms. In fact, as a general rule, if you want to send a text message, send an email; if you want to write an email, make a call; if you want to make call, meet in person; and if you want to meet in person, make it special.

If it's important enough to do, do it in person.

"OFF THE RECORD" COMMENTS ARE ALWAYS ON THE RECORD

When people hear the words "off the record," they imagine a news reporter turning off the tape recorder and telling the person being interviewed that no one will ever know what is being said. The problem, of course, is that there is no such thing as an "off the record" comment.

Even with a reporter, the "off the record" comment is made to the reporter, who will forever know what was said—the statement is out there.

In negotiations, you can never tell your opponent something without expecting it to go right back to the other side's key people.

In many mediations, I have had discussions with both sides' lawyers, and occasionally one lawyer would make a comment that was "off the record." Unless it is a tactical move, this comment simply shows your hand without gaining you anything in return.

You have to always assume that any information you convey to the other side or their agents will make its way to the decision makers.

On the other hand, if, as noted above, you actually *want* to reveal the information to the other side, then by labeling it "off the record" you make it secret—and it is simple human nature to want to be in on a secret. People love secrets, because being privy to a secret means you are part of an elite few. Beyond that, secret information has a tendency to be more trusted. This means that you can "leak" information to the other side with a supposed "off the record" comment.

GETTING ANGRY ONLY WEAKENS YOUR POSITION

There are many times during a negotiation when you may get frustrated and want to scream at the other side, "Why won't you just listen?" Sometimes anger arises from fear—fear that the deal won't go through; fear that you may lose an opportunity, or fear of the unknown. Anger, however, is never the answer. There is a saying that "anger is one letter short of danger." Nowhere is this statement more true than in the context of negotiations.

Anger can damage your negotiating power in many ways. First, as noted in an earlier section, people will know what buttons to push to make you angry.

Second, and more importantly, anger often closes you off to rational thinking. Instead of thinking of solutions to the mutual problem, you are now reacting emotionally. As my father-in-law, Billy, often says, "Empty barrels make the most noise."

Third, showing your anger essentially shows that you have lost control of the situation. You have lost power. Your opponents may be able to capitalize on the fact that you no longer control your own emotions.

Finally, your anger only serves to alienate the people around you. Indeed, most people's response to anger is to dig in their heels even further. Nevertheless, there are always people who feel that using negative emotions will cause the other side to capitulate. Although the "tantrum" tactic can occasionally work (see next chapter), in most cases the other side will simply refuse to participate in such conduct.

Recent research has also shown that using negative emotions such as anger can be bad for the bottom line. One study tested the influence of strategically displayed emotions, both positive and negative, on the outcome of negotiations. It found that the introduction of "negative" emotions significantly decreased the chance of the other side accepting an existing offer. Furthermore, when the opposing party was given a chance to counter the offer after negative emotions were introduced, the counters were more extreme and participants were less concerned whether the counter-proposal would be accepted. Negative emotions clearly affected the outcome of the negotiations.

If the other side frustrates you, stay calm. Before you react in anger, take ten deep breaths to relax and gain your perspective. If you can't take a breath, take a break. Just as with television, you can pause the action and replay the scene in your head to see what you want to do. By doing so you will be better able to arrive at a solution that gets you the best negotiated result.

ANGER BY THE OTHER SIDE CAN BE A MEANS TO CONTROL YOU

When someone shows anger, they often are honest about their emotions and may need a forum to express that anger. However, there are occasions where the other side is simply using anger (or other negative emotions) as an emotional negotiation tactic.

Watch for the fake temper tantrum. Be careful to determine whether the person having the outburst is trying to achieve something by it—is there a legitimate reason to be angry?

Negotiation temper tantrums often end as quickly as they start, just the way they do with children. People do not like to face anger and tantrums. As a result, some people will simply give in to the tantrum rather than face the difficult task of addressing why the tantrum took place in the first instance. The problem with using tantrums as a tactic is that it only works once, if at all. After the first time, the shock of the tantrum wears off on the other side.

Every time I think of tantrums in negotiations, I think of the child I once saw in the supermarket. The child wanted a piece of candy, and his mother wouldn't purchase it. Instantly, the child went into a rip-roaring tantrum, fell to the floor and cried hysterically. Still the mother did nothing but patiently watching her child. He continued with his tantrum for a full five minutes, during which the other patrons were avoiding the aisle while the mother didn't budge. Finally, he got up off the floor, wiped his nose and walked away sheepishly. As he walked off, I remember his mother's words: "I told you, tantrums don't pay."

Just as with the child's tantrum, if the other side is using a "tantrum" as a ploy, it's best to simply wait it out, just the way the mother did with her child. You can also respond that you do not appreciate the outburst and that you won't negotiate under those conditions.

When someone is shouting at me in a mediation, I simply and politely tell them that I would like to understand what they are saying so I can communicate it to the other side, but that it is hard for me to understand them when they shout or yell. I might also say that I can understand their feelings but am wondering whether they really want me to communicate that same anger to the other side, because if I did, it would probably destroy all negotiations. They generally say no, but that they just wanted to get it off their chest.

In either case, make sure to not simply react to someone's anger but instead to understand its root and then diffuse that situation in order to achieve the best environment in which to negotiate.

A PICTURE IS WORTH A THOUSAND WORDS

The famous saying that a picture is worth a thousand words is doubly true in negotiations. This does not mean, however, that you have to have a picture of everything. But if you have evidence that backs up your position, bring it to the negotiation.

When you are trying to prove a point, presenting the evidence that supports your argument is usually helpful. The majority of people are visual, meaning they are more easily persuaded by a picture than by simply being told of the evidence.

In one case where I represented a client who had been injured in a severe automobile accident, the entire issue hinged on whether the driver of the vehicle fell asleep at the wheel and drifted off the road, or whether a part in the axle broke, causing it to scrape against the ground, with the vehicle uncontrollably careening off the highway and down an embankment.

The debate over this issue raged on during the litigation, and at the mediation the defendant continued to argue that the plaintiff driver had fallen asleep at the wheel. I inquired whether, hypothetically, their perspective on the value of the case would be different, had the plaintiff driver not fallen asleep at the wheel. The defense said yes, but that they were sure that the plaintiff had indeed fallen asleep.

I then showed them, on my computer, the one picture of the scene of the accident that had been taken just moments after the accident. They thought nothing of it, because they had a hard copy of the picture and had seen it before. But as I zoomed in on the road, we could see a scrape in the pavement that ran all the way to the exact point where the car had gone off the road. The defense conceded the point and resolved the case.

By bringing the evidence for physical observation, you not only show that you are prepared for every contingency but also eliminate any debate that may occur when different memories recall different things.

SAY "I" AND NOT "YOU"

Many times in negotiations, things will get heated when the parties cannot easily agree. Too often parties will end up throwing accusations at each other: "You did not listen when I communicated that offer," or "You acted as if you didn't care." Instead of saying "you" did something, express it as an "I" phrase: "I feel that you didn't listen to my full proposal," or "I feel as if you don't want this deal to work."

Negotiations are often difficult enough without having to feel that someone is accusing you. In that context "you" becomes a fighting word that is very likely to put your opponent on the defensive.

It is helpful to remember that whenever we judge ourselves, we judge our actions, but when we judge others, we judge their intentions.

Take an example from the television show *Living With Ed*. Ed Begley Jr. has a reality TV show where he makes his house and others' environmentally responsible. On one episode, Ed sees that his wife loves his office chair, so he decides to get her another, identical chair, so that she has one of her own. His wife appreciates the gift but immediately questions her husband's motives. Instead of judging his action of giving a gift, she immediately judged his intentions as being self-serving. The same happens daily in negotiations.

By using "I" and not "you," you can let the other side know how you feel. It is much easier for your opponent to understand your position when they don't feel defensive.

DEADLINE DO'S AND DON'TS

A lot of negotiators will tell you never to disclose a deadline. That view, however, can be shortsighted. While it can be true that disclosing a deadline is a mistake, there are times when it's the right thing to do. The reality is that creating or disclosing a deadline depends on the circumstances.

At the very beginning of negotiations, it is usually not advisable to establish a deadline, since by doing so you are in essence telling the other side that you may not be as committed to the negotiations as they are.

In one case I mediated, both parties had flown in from out of town. I had scheduled a full day to mediate for them. One party stated very early in the negotiations, before any progress had been made, that they had to leave by 3 p.m. to catch a flight. This got the other side angry, because they felt that their opponents weren't committed to the process and had come to the mediation in bad faith.

But sometimes it is important to reveal deadlines. If negotiations are stalled or progressing very slowly, the imposition of a deadline can help the parties get to the point faster.

For example, most mediations that are scheduled with me are either a half-day or full day. When the parties know that they only have a half-day to resolve their dispute, they will often make faster concessions.

If you do have a deadline, it may make sense at some point during the negotiations to disclose it. According to Professor Don Moore at Carnegie Mellon University, the failure to disclose your deadline will eventually place you at a disadvantage—you will be forced to make concessions based upon your deadline, but your opponent won't.

No matter what the deadline, though, people have a tendency to make more concessions the closer they are to the deadline. In business there is the 80/20 rule, which states that 80 percent of the work gets done by 20 percent of the people and 80 percent of your work is accomplished in 20 percent of the time. The same is true in negotiations: Often 80 percent of the concessions are made in the last 20 percent of the time.

DEMONSTRATE THAT THE OTHER SIDE HAS SOMETHING TO LOSE FROM NOT MAKING THE DEAL

It is always nice to find ways that will show the other side that there are benefits to negotiating with you. But you should also make sure to show the other side what they can lose by *not* making a deal with you.

According to Robert Cialdini's book *Influence: Science and Practice*, people are more motivated by the thought of losing something than by the thought of gaining something. Many researchers have studied the framing of issues as "loss" or "gain" and have found time and time again that loss plays a powerful role in decision making. A 1994 study in *Organizational Behavior and Human Decision Processes*, for example, found that the prospect of having year-end losses was more likely to influence the decisions of managers than the chance that they could experience gains.

So, when you are trying to convince the other side to consider your proposal, make sure to provide arguments and reasons that illustrate the risk of loss.

For example, lately people have been discussing environmental awareness, and more and more companies are showing that they are "green." But how do you sell green to a business or consumer?

In my experience trying to sell the concept of going green, most people don't react when you inform them of the environmental benefits. However, when you explain how they stand to lose money if they *don't* go green, they start to react. In fact, on every occasion where I have pitched the simple concept of switching lights to compact fluorescent bulbs and explained that people were losing money because of the cost of electricity for other lighting types, people have changed their bulbs. On the other hand, when I tell them they could save money by changing their bulbs, fewer people are motivated to change.

A 1988 study investigated this very principle. The study framed an issue worth 50 cents a day as either a savings or a loss. Half the homeowners were told how much money they could save by fully insulating their homes; the other half were told how much they could lose if they didn't insulate their homes.

The study found that 150 percent more people agreed to insulate their homes under the "loss" language than under the "gain" language. According to Cialdini, "It was the same 50 cents, but people are more mobilized into action by the idea of losing something."

In addition to telling people about benefits, never forget to tell them what they can lose if they don't negotiate with you.

HELP THE OTHER SIDE SAVE FACE

Face-saving refers to allowing the other side to maintain a good public image, regardless of the circumstances.

According to the book *Nixon's Ten Commandments of Leadership and Negotiation: His Guiding Principles of Statecraft*, one of President Nixon's commandments was "Always leave your adversary a face-saving line of retreat." The book describes several international conflicts and negotiations where Nixon and his team allowed other world leaders to save face, resulting in benefits for the United States.

In business, allowing the other side to save face also has its benefits. Imagine an employee who is being terminated due to lack of performance. If that employee is not given a way to save face, he could end up suing for wrongful termination; or perhaps the employee tries to sabotage you or goes to a competitor and reveals trade secrets. But if, instead of annihilating the employee's morale, you allow him a way out, you have made a friend out of the employee instead of an enemy.

Even a small or insignificant act of face-saving can be invaluable. In the 1970s, the U.S. was trying to persuade Japan to revalue its currency because of trade deficits. The U.S. requested a 17-percent revaluation of the yen. The Japanese finance minister, however, refused to address the American proposal. He canceled his meeting with the American treasury secretary and attempted to avoid making concessions.

The U.S. treasury secretary later learned from the Japanese deputy finance minister that 17 percent was unacceptable because a prior finance minister had been assassinated after agreeing to a 17-percent revaluation. The treasury secretary then proposed a 16.9-percent revaluation, which was immediately accepted by the Japanese. The difference in the new proposal was insignificant but was symbolically crucial to allow the Japanese to save face.

INCORPORATE THE OTHER SIDE'S PROPOSAL IN YOUR COUNTER

If you can, try to see if you can incorporate some aspect of the other side's proposal into your counter-proposal. That way the other side will view your counter as being closer to their own terms than if you presented the same information but within the context of your own proposal.

In addition, because of the concept of reactive devaluation (see earlier chapter), people have a tendency to devalue something coming from their opponent. By the same token people value their own ideas more. By essentially accepting the framework from the other side, you are taking advantage of the other side's belief that what they proposed is better.

Finally, by accepting some of what the other side has offered, you are setting the stage for asking them to accept something that you will offer at a later date. As discussed earlier, there is an inherent feeling of reciprocity or obligation that we experience when we are given a gift. Here, you have given the gift of acceptance.

In one mediation involving trademark infringement, the defendant suggested that the parties agree to work within a range of $250,000 to $500,000. The plaintiffs were OK with a final number at the higher end of that range. Instead of countering with a different proposal, the plaintiffs agreed with the range but countered that they would not be willing to meet the defendant in the middle of the range. They accepted the other side's terms while simultaneously conveying their own position. Eventually, at the end of the negotiation, the plaintiffs told the defendant that they "have accepted your range, we now need you to accept our final proposal, because this is the bottom line." The defendant accepted.

CARE (BUT NOT TOO MUCH)

Obviously it is important to care about the outcome of the negotiation. However, you should never care too much, because if you do, the other side will realize that and use it against you.

By appearing to not care too much, you place your opponent at a disadvantage. Do you want the deal? Do you not? Are you going to walk away? If you show that you don't care that much, the other side gets more interested.

In fact, this technique is often used in dating—if a woman is interested in a man, she will feign disinterest, which in turn makes the man more interested in her. (The same principle seems to work vice versa.) You see this in the movies all the time.

Pretend that your negotiation is simply a game. Even if the deal falls apart, so what? By taking this attitude, you will be less stressed when negotiating the deal, and in the end you will get better results.

Most people worry that if they don't care enough, they won't do the best possible job and, therefore, not get the best possible deal.

One of the factors that will help you not to care too much is knowing your alternatives. If you enter a negotiation with a supplier, knowing that three other suppliers can provide you with the same product for a reasonable price, you won't care too much if you don't strike a bargain with this one. Knowing your alternatives will help you be a better negotiator.

So go ahead and negotiate, and in the famous words of singer Bobby McFerrin, "Don't worry, be happy."

BE CAREFUL ABOUT SPLITTING THE DIFFERENCE

Everyone knows the strategy of splitting the difference. This technique is used when the two sides are at the end of their negotiating rope and one side says, "Why don't we split the difference?" For example, if Joe and Sally are negotiating the sale of a refrigerator, and Joe says that his price is $100, and Sally says that her offer is $50, splitting the difference would bring the price to $75.

However, except for the most simple of cases, this technique can backfire and cause you to lose money. Take Joe and Sally's example. Let's say, Sally proposes to split the difference—that means she will agree to pay $75.

Joe might respond, "So you would agree to pay $75?"

Sally replies, "Yes, but only if you agree to $75."

Joe replies, "OK, let me think about it." He may even say, "My wife has the final say-so, since she does the books at our house."

Later he comes back and says, "I thought about it, and I can't agree to $75. I really think $100 is the price. But rather than fight you over it, I would be willing to compromise and sell it for $87.50." What Joe did was to "split the split." Now Sally is faced with the tough choice of having to walk away from the deal for only a $12.50 difference.

If you think you would be willing to split the difference, ask in a hypothetical way if the other side would be willing to split the difference. Or use the "limited authority" excuse as a way to split the difference by stating that you would recommend to your boss to split the difference, but you would have to know that the other side would accept such a split before you recommended it.

Because the parties often have invested a lot of time and energy into the process, they might find it hard to turn down the offer and walk away with nothing.

IN GOOD CONSCIENCE, I MUST SAY "NO"

During a negotiation, it is sometimes necessary to say no in order to get to a yes that is acceptable to you. One way to say no is to rely on principles that cannot be disputed or questioned.

Let's say your close friend wants you to go with him to a stage show that you despise, and you don't want to go. If you simply say no, your friend might get offended. And if you say that you can't because you're busy, he might reply, "Well, it's a six-week engagement, so we can do it another night." However, if you use a principle that he cannot object to, you can say no gracefully. For example, you might say, "I can't go because I object to the message of the production," or "I can't go because I boycott the director for his views on human rights."

The key is to give a reason that is personal to you and involves a deep-seated principle behind not wanting to participate.

In negotiations, you can use the same technique. For example, if an employee is asking for a raise, you might respond that you cannot give a raise at this time because it's your personal policy to only issue raises at review time.

Remember, when saying no, the reason must be true. And if your principle is based on an event, make sure the event is true. Don't lie. For example, when I was 18 years old, a credit card company refused to give me credit even though I had very good credit. Ever since that time, I have refused to use that company for anything and have never conducted business with it. There have been many opportunities involving that company, but each time I have refused on the grounds that I boycotted that specific company because of what happened when I was younger. The story is true, and no one can question my own, personal motives.

WE'VE NEVER DONE THAT BEFORE

Another tactic that you can use to counter proposals you don't want to consider is to answer that you "have never done that before." This comment goes directly to the concept of precedent—you have never done it before and are not likely to do it now.

Sometimes this response can place you in the position of informing the other side what you actually can consider. On other occasions, the person on the receiving end of your comment might ask what you have done in the past, giving you the opportunity to say what terms are acceptable to you.

In one case, an insurance company was negotiating over the value of a rear-end car accident with minor injuries, often known as "soft-tissue" injuries. The plaintiff wanted far more than the insurance company was willing to pay. The insurance representative explained to the plaintiff, "We have had a team of people look at this case. The nature of your injuries is typical for a car accident of this nature. We have never paid what you ask for in these types of cases. Now, if you have something that takes your case out of the normal realm, we would be happy to consider it." The insurance company skillfully used this technique as well as identifying norms and framed the negotiation to its advantage.

ASK QUESTIONS

Questions are probably the negotiator's most powerful tool. Questions provide you with information. Speaking without asking questions only reveals information. The famous French author Voltaire once said, "Judge others by their questions rather than their answers." As a general rule, the person who asks the questions is the one in control of the negotiation.

Think about a witness on the stand being cross-examined by an attorney. Who is in control of the situation? The attorney. The attorney has the ability to ask any question, whereas the witness can only answer the questions before him. If the attorney does not want a fact to become known, all she needs to do is not ask the question.

In cross-examinations as well as negotiations, asking the right questions is a combination of art and science. The wrong question or, more specifically, the wrong way to ask a question can lead to a negotiating mishap. Fortunately, there are some guidelines to asking good questions during negotiations.

There are two types of questions: open-ended and closed-ended. Both serve a purpose at different times during a negotiation.

Open-ended questions require a broad answer and cannot be answered simply by saying yes or no. They start with who, what, where, when, why, or how. (For example, "When do you think the project will be completed?") The answering party has no choice but to provide some specifics.

There are several types of open-ended questions. There are those that identify thought patterns, such as "Why do you think that?" or "What do you think about reducing expenses?" There are open-ended questions about feelings, such as "How do you feel about this?" There are those questions that ask about process or procedure, such as "What needs to be done next?" There are also open-ended questions that assume facts, such as "After we complete the negotiations over the price, when do you want to talk about the terms?" Each of these open-ended questions can be used at different times of the negotiation.

Closed-ended questions or leading questions should only be used if you want to lead the person to the answer that you desire. They are not used to obtain information. For example, "Don't you agree that we should look at objective data as a basis for this negotiation?" Or, "Wouldn't you agree that the market conditions will cause the price to go down?" Isn't time of delivery the most important aspect of this deal?" Each of these questions makes a statement of what you believe implicitly in the question.

NEGOTIATING
WITH A CLIENT

Many negotiations involve a client. That client could be your boss because you represent your employer's interest; it could be an individual you represent, or a member of your family. Any of the strategies that have been discussed throughout can be used with clients.

However, there are additional issues you should consider when negotiating with a client. This section will focus on the specific issues that are involved when you negotiate with a client.

SHARE WEAKNESSES AND STRENGTHS WITH CLIENTS

Your client is probably not as familiar with the subject of the negotiation as you are. Although your client may be aware of the general nature of the subject, you have spent more time preparing for the negotiation and have more knowledge about this process than he or she does. Make sure that you meet with your client beforehand and prepare him or her about the specific issues involved in the negotiation. Provide him or her with all the information about the strengths and weaknesses of the case.

Trial consultants recommend that you should always be the first to disclose any weakness in your case to the jury. This ensures that you have credibility with the jury. The consultants often explain the concept like a vaccination. With a vaccine, you give the patient a small dose of the harmful virus so that the body can build an immunity. Telling the jury first about your weakness helps to immunize the jury to larger claims that may be made about your case by the other side. Such disclosure, however, requires advance preparation and a full understanding of your own case.

Not only will such preparation help your client make the right decision, but it also makes you look good. I have been in several mediations where I informed one side about the weakness of its case, and the client turned to his attorney and said something along the lines of "Why is it that I'm hearing this for the first time? Did we know this?"

By fully briefing your client, you will help them feel more confident in your abilities. Your advice is more credible because you were already aware of the complete situation.

Finally, preparing your client for the good, the bad, and the ugly also allows them to realize that the deal they end up with is good. If the client goes in thinking everything is rosy, a compromise resolution won't seem like such a good deal.

You've prepared yourself for the negotiation—don't forget to prepare the client.

TAP INTO YOUR SIXTH SENSE

Every time I go on a cruise, there is a magician doing a show; and every good magician has a trick where he demonstrates his mastery of ESP, or extra-sensory perception—and every time he mentions the acronym "ESP," a huge echo reverberates through the room. Through his ESP, this magician can tell the future; he can read minds; and he knows where to find a certain card out of a deck.

We know that the magician's trick is just that: a trick. Nevertheless, it works like a charm every time. You can do the same magic with your client. Tap into your sixth sense and let the client know what will happen during the negotiation.

By telling the client what will happen in the future, you let her know that you actually know what you're talking about. I know, this is a shocker to you. But it's true—you do know what you're talking about. And now, so does your client.

In most mediations, at some point during the day, I will use my ESP to let the client know what is going to happen. Often I will predict that the other side is going to make a first offer that is, in the client's eyes, outrageous and that she probably will want to walk out at that moment. I explain that the other side will take about an hour before they make their first proposal and that they will probably argue one of several arguments. To the client's amazement, all those things usually come true. Now she confirms her belief that I know what I'm talking about, without my ever having to list my credentials. Seeing is believing, as they say.

After seeing that I seem to have a good grip on the subtleties of this unusual environment, the client is much more willing to listen to my advice and to accept my recommendations.

You have a lot of experience in your field. Demonstrating that experience by identifying possible future actions or events allows you a greater opportunity to help your client make the right decision. So, next time you have a client, think how you can use ESP.

HAVE YOUR CLIENT ARGUE FOR THE OTHER SIDE

Sometimes you may have difficulty getting your client to fully understand the true nature of the other side's position. Many times, the other side may have a very good point that your client is just not willing to recognize. On those occasions, it is helpful for you to ask your client to advocate the other side's argument.

By vocally arguing the other side's position, your client is in a small way committing to that position. She is making the claim that the other's side position is valid and correct. Studies have shown that even small commitments such as simply making a public or vocal statement in favor of a particular position can help a person commit to that position.

In one study, students were asked to estimate the size of a line. Some were asked to make a public written statement disclosed to others about the size of a line, a second group made a private written statement, and a third group was only asked to keep the size in their head. Later, the students were told that the size that they had estimated was in fact wrong. The students who had not made a public or private statement about the size of the line were willing to reconsider their estimate; the students who had written private estimates were less willing to change the estimate, and the students who had written the public statement were extremely unwilling to change their initial estimate. All because they had made a public commitment.

Once the client has made the public statement in favor of the other side's argument, it's helpful for you to compliment her argument and her ability to persuade. Studies have also shown that people are affected by what other people think of them. Specifically, they tend to believe facts about themselves when other people believe those facts too. Your complimenting them on their argument will make them more likely to accept that argument, because they believe that they are believed by others.

Having your client argue for the other side provides a small but powerful way to help convince your client that she needs to negotiate for optimum results.

NEVER STATE THAT YOU HAVE CONTROL OVER YOUR CLIENT

Many times during the negotiation, the other side's representative will ask you whether you have "control over your client" or whether "your boss is going to have a problem with the deal as proposed." These questions are intended to find out who has to be convinced of the other side's position. In other words, "If we convince you of this argument or position, is your client going to be an obstacle to getting the deal done?" No matter what your position or authority, if you are representing someone, never state that you have complete control or complete decision-making power.

The moment you say that you have control or authority, you lose all control. Now, all the other side has to do is convince you, and the deal is done.

In one case I mediated, the parties had been making progress throughout the mediation. At one point late in the game, the defendant's attorney took me aside and told me that his client was having difficulty accepting the final terms proposed by the plaintiff. He said that he had done everything he could but he couldn't control what his client would do. He asked me to communicate this information to the other side.

When the other side heard about this wildcard issue, they asked to speak to the defendant's attorney. The attorneys had a meeting where the defendant's attorney explained that his client was a wildcard who, all along, hadn't wanted to enter into negotiations and that he, the attorney, had had to convince him. He finally explained that his client had gone over the edge and would not accept the plaintiff's final proposal, so he asked the plaintiff's attorney if he had control over his client and whether the client would do what his attorney recommended.

The plaintiff's attorney responded that he had the ability to persuade his client to accept terms that he deemed acceptable. The plaintiff's attorney, however, was now sufficiently scared that the deal might fall apart and that the many hours spent in mediation would be wasted. So he said, "If I can get my client to accept your last proposal, will your client still be willing to do the deal?" The defense attorney responded, "I don't know. I could have said yes an hour ago, but now I don't know. But are you saying that you would accept what my client previously proposed?"

The plaintiff's attorney responded, "Yes, I think so. But let me check." Minutes later, after having spoken with the plaintiff, the attorney confirmed that he would be willing to accept the defendant's last offer if it was still on the table. Ten minutes later, we had a deal.

No one will know, and the defense attorney certainly won't reveal whether his client's "wildcard" status was real or a tactical ploy. But the fact that the defense attorney could not control his client helped them gain terms that were favorable to them.

This tactic is also helpful in that it draws on the good-cop/bad-cop strategy—the attorney or representative becomes the good cop who would agree to the terms, but his client, the bad cop, is a wildcard who won't agree. Since the client is the one with the right to make the decision, even if it is irrational, the representative comes out smelling like a rose.

Never say you have complete control. Always reserve the right to play the game with a wildcard.

SEPARATE THE CLIENT FROM THE REPRESENTATIVE

Sometimes there is disagreement between a client and his representative on how to negotiate a case. If you suspect that there is a crack in the other side's joint position, try to get the representative away from the client for a brief period of time so that you can have a frank conversation with the agent.

One thing to consider in this case are the representative's motives. You will find that they differ greatly from the client's. Many representatives simply want to keep their job. Others want to shine in front of their boss or client. Examine those motives for a potential break in the unified front that can be used in the negotiation.

The agent may give you valuable information that can help get a resolution. Or you may find that the agent agrees with many of the things that you have proposed, but the client doesn't. By separating the client from the representative, you also create an opportunity for the representative to become your ally in achieving a resolution.

In one case, the parties had reached an impasse. Neither side's client was willing to make any further concessions. The plaintiff was asking $300,000, and the defendants were offering $200,000. This was huge progress, given that the plaintiff had started at over $1 million and the defendant at $10,000. But now each side had reached its bottom line position.

I asked both side's representatives to meet with me, and I asked them what was preventing us from getting the case resolved. Each representative told me that they would like to resolve the case, but that the clients were unwilling to go any further. Both representatives knew that the case would be very costly to litigate and neither side had any guarantees—and if they lost, the respective clients would be even angrier than if they arrived at a less-than-ideal settlement.

It became clear to me that both representatives were essentially willing to work towards a compromise but were hampered by their clients' positions. We had the situation that Sun Tzu, the ancient Chinese philosopher, had referred to when he said, "When enemies are in the same boat and are caught by a storm, they will come to each other's assistance just as the left hand helps the right." What we had was a great storm and the enemies were coming to each other's assistance.

Both sides' representatives were allied in trying to get their respective clients to compromise a little bit more. After a short period of brainstorming between the two new allies, we were able to find a way to create a compromise both sides agreed to.

You never know what will happen when you get the client away from the representative.

IF YOUR CLIENT MADE A MISTAKE, FIND A SCAPEGOAT

If your client makes a mistake that is apparent to the other side, don't let the client take the fall; find a scapegoat instead. If the other side blames your client, it can cause severe damage to the negotiation process. But if, on the other hand, the other side believes that an agent or an employee is at fault, then the mistake is easier to forgive.

In one case we had scheduled a mediation to take place for four hours. On the day of the mediation, the plaintiff, her counsel and the defendant's attorney arrived at the mediation, ready to negotiate, but the defendant never showed up. It turned out that the defendant had forgotten to put the mediation on his calendar. The plaintiff and her lawyer were extremely angry and felt insulted that they had wasted their time and money to come to the mediation. The situation was getting ugly, and the plaintiff even threatened to escalate the lawsuit, which would have cost everyone a lot more money.

In a very smart move, the attorney for the defendant told the plaintiff that it must have been his office's fault for not sending the letter informing the client of the mediation. Based on what the attorney had told me earlier in confidence, I knew this not to be true, but he was falling on the proverbial sword and making himself the scapegoat.

This helped calm the situation down. The plaintiff was still angry, but the defendant's lawyer said, "I'm really sorry this happened. My assistant failed to send the notice to the client. I don't want you to feel that we don't take this case seriously. We do. To prove that we want to try to resolve this case, we will agree to pay for the next mediation session, and I will make sure that my secretary lets the client know of the mediation." This placated the plaintiff, and she recognized that people make mistakes and agreed to another session. In fact, she even asked the defendant's attorney not to be too hard on the secretary.

Remember, if your client makes a mistake in front of the other side, it wasn't your client's fault.

PREVIEW THE PROCESS FOR YOUR CLIENT

Many times the client will enter the negotiation and not know anything about the process itself. Often, this happens when you are dealing with people who have not experienced your particular situation. Make sure to advise the client of the entire process. Explain the timing, the meaning of the process, how things will proceed, and other procedural issues. A client who is less stressed is more likely to make smart decisions.

In most litigated mediations involving individuals, as opposed to corporate entities, the individuals are new to the litigation process and have never gone through a mediation. Those individuals are often scared and unsure about how the process will go.

I make it a point to explain to them what to expect during the day. I will inform them that the process takes time, that I may conduct shuttle diplomacy going from room to room, that there may be a lot of emotions involved, that we may have to speak with people privately or in joint session, and many other such procedural issues.

By explaining the situation, I put the individuals at ease about the process and show that I can be trusted because I have been transparent about how everything will work.

Many times when something happens in the course of the mediation that I previously explained, the parties will tell me that I told them it would be like this. That simple act of explaining the process gives me instant credibility. And because I helped them overcome some of their fears about the process, they are usually grateful to me. All of these things, as previously noted, will serve to help you in negotiations.

Finally, by explaining the process, you will prevent your client from getting impatient or coming to the wrong conclusion based upon a lack of knowledge. For example, if your client knows that the other side is going to provide an outrageous initial offer that nobody expects you to accept, the client will be able to shrug it off, instead of getting angry, when that offer is actually made.

Just as a person shines a flashlight into an alleyway to preview the path ahead, a preview of the process will help your client travel down the negotiation path.

MAKE THE OTHER SIDE'S REPRESENTATIVE LOOK GOOD

When negotiating, it is good to remember that it is a small world. Everybody knows someone you'll know. And word spreads quickly in every industry. This means that when you are negotiating with someone, you are actually negotiating with everyone that person knows. Your reputation will precede you in many negotiations. It is also important to remember that everyone has to justify their job. If you can make the other side's representative look good, it will go a long way towards helping you foster good relations not only with this one party but perhaps with many others.

When making proposals or deals, try to describe the concessions that you have made because of the other side's representative. If possible, give the other side the impression that their representative is really protecting their interests.

Making the other side's representative look good will make it easier to arrive at a deal, because she won't have to worry that by presenting your proposal she could be out of a job soon.

In addition, as stated above, the other side's representative knows a lot of people. Your interaction in this negotiation could very well affect your future interactions with other people. Which one would you prefer, the reputation of being tough but fair or of being a jerk?

Take a case I mediated recently. I had never mediated with any of the parties before, nor had the parties interacted with each other before.

Curiously, though, one side was extremely antagonistic towards the other right from the start. As the day continued, I could tell that the same party continued to be very guarded and would not open up to the other side, despite several overtures by the other side.

When I got into a private session with the antagonistic party, I asked them what was bothering them. They responded, "We have heard of these guys before. We know that they play dirty and won't make any concessions. So we don't want to make reasonable offers because we are worried that they won't respond in kind." This was a recipe for disaster.

The rest of the day was spent developing trust between the two parties just so they could negotiate a little better. Remember, if you are going to be a competitive negotiator, try to avoid winning the battle while losing the war.

GIVE THE REPRESENTATIVE TALKING POINTS TO JUSTIFY THEIR RECOMMENDATIONS TO THE CLIENT

When the negotiation concludes and the representatives agree to the terms of the deal, that does not mean the negotiations are over. The representatives must go to their respective clients and justify the deal. When the representative goes back to her client, she needs to be able to justify why the deal is worth agreeing to.

Sometimes, it is helpful to ask the other representative what they need from you to sell the deal to their client.

In one case involving litigation over the purchase of real estate, the representatives had worked hard to arrive at an agreement that would be amenable to both sides. The case centered on the buyer accusing the seller of failing to disclose defects and the seller denying that he knew about the defects at the time of the sale.

The agreement determined the amount the seller had to pay to the buyer for repairs to the property. The seller's attorney asked the buyer's attorney for specific documents that would show the defects. The buyer happened to have photographs taken the day of the move that showed water leaks from windows and stains on ceilings. The photographs were dated and were hard to dispute. The seller's attorney was able to use those photographs to sell the proposal to the seller.

The deal isn't done when you agree to it. The hard part is selling the deal to the client.

USING A NEUTRAL MEDIATOR

Many negotiations involve a mediator or a third party who tries to assist the parties in resolving their disputes. In fact, there are many people who can act as mediators in disputes—family members, neighbors, priests or rabbis, administrators, coworkers, lawyers, judges, or trained mediators.

The mediator's role is not to judge or to say who is right or wrong but to help the parties get to the core of the dispute and the problems created by the dispute. Mediators try to help the parties devise their own solutions. The purpose of mediation is to give the parties an opportunity to meet and try to resolve the situation in a protective setting.

Negotiations take on a very different dynamic when a third party is involved. Not only does the mediator's personality come into play, but many times use of a neutral intermediary through which to communicate saves you from having to talk directly with the other side.

Although many of the strategies identified in this book so far also apply to the third-party/mediation context, some strategies are unique to mediation and deserve special attention.

YOU BOTH MUST HAVE TRUST IN THE MEDIATOR

For mediation to be effective, the parties must have at least a basic level of trust in the mediator. Without it, the mediator will be hampered in his or her abilities to help find a resolution. Even if that trust extends only as far as having the confidence that the mediator won't do something to harm either side. By having trust in the mediator, the parties can trust the process, which means they're willing to share information with other parties and with the mediator, which helps the mediator get to the bottom of the problem and assist in finding a resolution.

When you discuss the idea of mediation, it is important to establish that the other party feels comfortable with the chosen mediator. If you recommend the mediator, you should be prepared to give the other side reasons to also feel comfortable with that person. Make sure to provide information—whether it be website, resume, credentials, reputation, or other indicators of credibility, that the other side can confirm. Encourage the other side to speak with the mediator without you. The more comfortable with the mediator you can make the other side, the better the chances for a successful mediation.

There are several things that will develop trust in a mediator before the mediation: reputation, past performance, and substantial knowledge of the field or area. Consider how a potential mediator fares in these areas when making a recommendation.

Trust is a critical ingredient in mediation. Beyond the trust that must be established before the mediation, there is the trust that is established during the mediation. Ultimately, as Victorian writer George MacDonald once said, "to be trusted is a greater compliment than to be loved."

HELP THE MEDIATOR UNDERSTAND YOUR SIDE

As Jerry Maguire in the movie by the same name said, "Help me; help me help you." Jerry's words could apply to mediation. Help the mediator be prepared to help you. Days to weeks before the mediation, send a brief summary of the case to the mediator. The more complex the case or dispute, the more detailed your summary should be. If you can, you should also try to send source materials and documents.

For example, if your case involves a car accident, send pictures of the car and the scene as well as police and medical reports. If you can, you should also cite those documents in your summary. For example, you might explain in your summary that the accident happened at 5th and Wilshire Blvd, and add, "See Exhibit A, the Police Report."

Providing such evidence and referring to it helps the mediator quickly understand the issues. It also has an additional benefit—it gives you credibility. It shows the mediator that you are prepared for the negotiation, that you know the critical facts and issues, and that you are prepared to back up your claims.

The perfect example of preparation and backup happened when I was in trial once. I was cross-examining a doctor about his opinions regarding the cause of a condition. At the time, I was in my early 30s and the doctor was in his late 50s. The doctor felt he knew more about medicine than I did, which was true.

I had previously taken the doctor's deposition, which recorded his testimony in a booklet by a court reporter. I had also gone to the library and checked out every medical textbook discussing the doctor's specialty. I may not have known medicine like the doctor, but I knew how he'd appear to the jury.

The doctor was very cocky when he took the stand. In the beginning, he wouldn't answer the questions the way I wanted, and would contradict everything I said. Realizing this, I started to ask the doctor questions that he had previously answered in his deposition. Every time he answered the question in a way that was different from his deposition testimony, I made a show of raising my hand and pulling out the deposition transcript, getting to the page of the doctor's testimony on the topic, and asking the doctor to read his own prior testimony, which contradicted his current testimony. After going through this process about 10 times, the doctor started to look at where my hand was going before he started to answer the question—and proceeded to answer the questions properly.

Then I started to ask questions that were not in his deposition, at which point it became obvious that the doctor was thinking he had me. He started to stray again and avoided answering—so I brought out a very thick textbook, whose author I identified as being from Harvard or some other prestigious medical school, and showed him where a professor of medicine disagreed with him on each specific question. Then I placed the book on the table in front of the doctor and asked the next question. By the end of my cross-examination, there were about 15 large textbooks in front of the doctor, and the jury was ignoring everything the doctor was saying about the medicine and wrote down everything I was saying.

I had built credibility with the neutral jury. I had demonstrated to them that every time I made a statement, I could back it up with hard evidence. The doctor, who was supposed to be the expert, showed himself to not be credible, because everything he said contradicted the hard evidence.

The same is true for you in a mediation. Make sure that everytime you make a statement, that you can back it up with evidence. Eventually, you will have built up enough credibility that every time you speak, the mediator will assume that you can back it up.

Help yourself by helping the mediator to help you.

HAVE THE MEDIATOR SUGGEST YOUR OFFER

In some mediations, especially those involving competitive negotiations, you may be willing to make a concession but be afraid to do so. If you show you are willing to make a concession, the other side might take advantage of it to elicit further concessions. In those circumstances, it is helpful to allow the mediator to suggest your concession as his or her idea instead of yours. Of course, it is important that you have implicit trust in the mediator to not reveal your strategy to the other side.

Let's take a negotiation in a litigated case involving trade secret violations. You represent Widget Corporation, which has been accused of stealing trade secrets from Acme, Inc. After several rounds of negotiations, you recognize that because the case is hotly contested, and because Acme is a competitor, there is very little trust among the parties. Your last offer to Acme was $200,000, while Acme's last demand was $450,000. You decide that you would be willing to pay $300,000 as a final price but are concerned that if you offer $300,000, Acme might simply use that as launch point for a higher price.

In that case, you could let the mediator know that you might be willing to pay more than $200,000. However, you also tell him that you are concerned that if the other side thinks the offer is coming from you, that they will reject it and counter-offer. You then suggest to the mediator that he present the offer as his idea. Many times, a mediator feels comfortable carrying such a message. He goes to Acme and asks them whether they'd be willing to accept $300,000 if he could get Widget to raise their offer.

In many cases, such a conversation is the key to getting resolution, especially in competitive cases.

INFORM THE MEDIATOR OF ANY SPECIAL NEEDS

On most occasions, you will have an opportunity either before or during the mediation to have a private conversation with the mediator. You should take that time to inform her of any special needs or issues that might arise.

For example, you might tell the mediator about the history of the dispute, any emotional issues that might be involved, any procedural issues that could affect the outcome of the case, or any applicable time constraints, to name a few.

By letting the mediator know of these dynamics, you can help her plan what needs to be done during the negotiation as well as how to orchestrate certain moves or discussions.

In one case, the attorney for the plaintiff called me before the mediation to let me know that his client was the father of a woman who had passed away due to a drug overdose. The father was accusing the woman's ex-husband of giving her the drugs and, in essence, causing her death. Obviously, this was a very emotional case. Right away I acknowledged that it might be very hard to have the parties in the same building, let alone the same room.

The attorney also told me that the court had urged the parties to go to mediation, but the father didn't want to. The father should resolve the case, but it was going to be difficult to convince him to do so.

This information gave me valuable information to help the mediation process. I made sure that the two parties arrived at different times and that they were in different rooms far apart from each other. I also made a special effort to understand the father's situation to be able to identify solutions.

Arming the mediator with information about the case beforehand can only serve to help you.

CONSIDER ASKING THE MEDIATOR TO MAKE A "MEDIATOR'S PROPOSAL"

Some mediations will last for many hours and still end up with an impasse. In those cases it is worthwhile to consider a mediator's proposal.

Many mediators are familiar with this concept, even though some parties to the negotiation process may not be. So let me explain the concept of a mediator's proposal.

A mediator's proposal is an offer to both sides, coming from the mediator, for an agreement that is beyond what either side has stated they are willing to consider. The mediator's proposal is to be made only if there is an impasse; if there is no impasse, this tool should not be used.

The mediator's proposal doesn't come from either of the parties, and neither of the parties can tell the mediator what the proposal should be. The proposal is intended to resolve the differences of the parties and often reflects the mediator's belief as to what might be a fair resolution given the circumstances.

The mediator's proposal is, in almost all cases, something that neither side likes or feels immediately comfortable with. It often suggests a resolution that is initially beyond both party's belief of what's acceptable.

The other important part of the mediator's proposal is the double-blind nature. This means that if one side said yes to the proposal but the other side said no, the "no" side would never know that the other side had said yes. All it would know is that there is no deal. This preserves both sides' negotiating position. If, on the other hand, both sides say yes, then you have a deal.

This technique can be very effective in helping the parties move away from their entrenched position and face-saving in that they did not make any offers beyond their final offer. Instead, they merely accepted the recommendation of the neutral third party.

ASK THE MEDIATOR QUESTIONS

Because much of the communication in a mediation may take place between the individual parties and the mediator, and not directly between the parties, it is hard for the parties to get a sense of "what is going on in the other room." It is, therefore, very helpful for a party to ask the mediator questions to gauge the mood and demeanor of the other party.

In essence, the mediator is the eyes and ears for both sides. You have to rely on him to be able to let you know what is going on and provide the reasons for why the other side acts in a certain manner. Questions to the mediator help you get that information so that you can make better decisions of your own.

Questions you may be asking include "What is the emotional state of the other side?"; "How did they react to my last offer?"; "Why did they do a certain thing?" and many more. In fact, many of the open-ended questions identified earlier can also be used with the mediator.

ASK FOR THE MEDIATOR'S RECOMMENDATIONS

You have asked the mediator to help you resolve the dispute. Don't be afraid to ask her advice as to what you should do next. You may know more about your case or product, but the mediator is probably getting a better idea of the circumstances of the parties and the mediation.

Asking for her recommendation helps you evaluate what she thinks might be a reasonable move or proposal, given what she heard and saw from the other side. Essentially, you can gauge how competitive or cooperative you need to be based on the mediator's recommendation.

For example, if you have a first offer from the other side and the mediator recommends that you counter well below that, you're in an entirely different negotiation than if the mediator tells you to make a counter-offer that's very close to the other side's offer.

Just because you ask for the advice of the mediator, however, doesn't mean you have to accept that advice. Just as with doctors, many people don't follow the advice of mediators. Nevertheless, just as with doctors, mediators are probably still going to give you their advice, and that advice can be valuable.

LET THE MEDIATOR EXPLAIN THE REALITY OF THE SITUATION TO YOUR CLIENT

One of the advantages of mediation is that the mediator can help you explain the realities of life, litigation, law, business, or the current situation to your client. If you have fully prepared your client, she has probably heard about much of this from you. But the question is, does the client, in her heart, believe what you said?

Allowing the mediator to reiterate what you have already told the client is very helpful in convincing the client. Advertising and marketing professionals will tell you that it takes at least seven exposures to an advertisement before the prospect will consider buying the product. You may have sent the message several times yourself, and the mediator's reinforcement of that message increases the likelihood of your client "buying the product."

Look at it from another perspective. The process of mediation is a learning process—each side is learning about the other side, either directly or through the mediator. When you studied geometry or algebra for the first time, and if you were anything like me, it took many repetitions for you to grasp its complexities. We shouldn't expect learning in mediation to be any different.

People learn at different paces and require different levels of repetition. Allowing the mediator to reiterate your points helps to reinforce the message that you have already given.

SHOULD YOU REVEAL A BOTTOM LINE TO THE MEDIATOR?

Should you reveal a bottom line number to the mediator? Unfortunately, there is no definitive answer. There are, however, some general guidelines.

First, it is generally advisable not to reveal a bottom line to the mediator, even in confidence, and especially early in the mediation. Revealing a bottom line simply sets you up for failure because you are now committed to a certain position. As noted earlier, those types of commitments tend to entrench people in their positions even when they are later found to be wrong.

Second, when you reveal your bottom line early, it defeats the purpose of the mediation, which should be about being flexible to adapt to the new information learned during the mediation process.

Third, giving the mediator a bottom line simply anchors the mediator to that number rather than flexibly allowing the number to move towards its natural destination. It is generally better to let the mediator guesstimate your bottom line based upon your moves during the negotiation.

If, however, you reach a point where you are no longer willing to negotiate, you may have to reveal your bottom line. At that point you might also consider revealing your bottom line so as not to mislead the mediator as to your true intentions.

A LITTLE BIT MORE

After you have negotiated the main points and both parties feel satisfied that they have arrived at a workable agreement, you might consider trying to get a little bit more to make the agreement a spectacular deal.

The following section is a little bit more about getting a little bit more.

ASK FOR SOMETHING NOT DIRECTLY RELATED TO THE NEGOTIATION

One of the important ways to get a little bit more is to ask for something that doesn't mean too much to either side and can easily be accomplished. The little bit more that you seek should be something that is not directly related to the subject of negotiations. And your chances are best when everybody invested a lot of time and is ready to close the deal and move on.

Many people call this tactic "nibbling." In the same way an animal nibbles at food, the negotiator nibbles for small concessions. This can be a powerful technique partly because people are often the most vulnerable when the deal has been struck and they don't want to lose it at the last minute. In addition, it could appear mean-spirited to refuse the other side something so small.

Nibbling happens in every context. An example of nibbling in the context of a home purchase is to include approval of a professional home inspection report contingency in the sales contract and then to negotiate repairs or rebates for damage found during the inspection.

In the car sales business, it is the undercoating or the floor mats; in the appliance business, it is the free delivery or free accessories; in the hotel business, it might be the upgraded room; in the shipping business, the number of days it takes to ship; and in the services business, the free consultation.

Oftentimes, the nibbles will keep coming until you put a stop to them. However, by the time you feel compelled to stop the nibbles, you have probably given away quite a bit.

So if you want to get a little bit more, go ahead and nibble away.

PUT IT IN WRITING

This technique can be used as a nibbler or if you are close to getting a deal but need that extra push to get a resolution. Most people think of putting something in writing just to enforce an agreement, but you can also put an offer in writing to try to get that little bit extra.

Generally, you must be very close to getting a deal or at least in the later stages of negotiations. You may suspect that the other side's final offer is coming and that you probably won't like it. During most of your negotiations, you have been communicating your offers orally. In response to a move by the other side, you will now put your next offer in writing with some level of formality, whether it be a deal memo, stipulation of agreement, settlement agreement, or real estate counter-offer. In that written document, you place the terms that you are willing to abide by, and sign the document.

This technique is similar to what you might see in a car dealership, where the sales manager, after negotiating with you all day, writes a number on a piece of paper and initials it. He then hands you the paper and tells you, "This is the best we can do."

In one case, the parties had negotiated orally all day. At the end of the day, the plaintiff was asking for $275,000, and the defendant was willing to pay $250,000. Nobody had communicated that they were at their bottom line. The defendant, however, indicated to me privately that it was amenable with any deal between the two numbers but that it wanted to sweeten the deal a little bit more. The defendant then wrote an offer on my standard two-page form for settlement agreements. Both the defendant and his attorney then signed the offer—it was for $259,000. That offer was presented to the plaintiff and her attorney, who contemplated it for about 20 minutes before accepting it. The case was resolved.

Putting your final offer or close to your final offer in writing can have a profound impact on changing the dynamic of the negotiation. The terms of the offer may be the same, but the way it is communicated can change the way the other side perceives it.

MODIFY MINOR PROVISIONS SUCH AS DELIVERY OR DATE OF PAYMENT

Let's say that you have been negotiating over such terms as price, quantity, delivery, and payment terms. If the other side is focusing on one of the terms in particular, such as price, you can grudgingly accept the price with a compromise in the delivery date or payment terms. You may have even agreed to that minor issue earlier in your discussion, but now you can reopen the negotiation on it because you are accepting the other side's terms on something that's important (to them).

In one case, the parties had been negotiating over the sale of a business interest. Jack was buying out the interest of his former partner, George, rather than force a dissolution of the business. George, who was focusing on the dollar value of his time and services, insisted that Jack pay $125,000 for George's half interest in the partnership. Jack felt that $125,000 was on the high end of the acceptable range. The parties had previously agreed that whatever the amount ended up being, the payment would be made in three equal monthly payments.

In order to make the deal happen, Jack announced that "I don't agree with the price, and I think the market value for the half share is inflated because of artificial conditions affecting fair market value. However, George, we have worked together a long time. Maybe we will work together in the future. Therefore, I am going to agree with the $125,000, with one small caveat: I will need an extra two months to get the money together and finance it."

George was now faced with having been given a major concession on the price tied to a minor concession on the terms of payment—the change in terms was worth about $3,000 to $5,000 in interest and opportunity-cost savings to Jack. George accepted the offer.

By modifying a small term at the end, you can create a small advantage.

EXPLAIN THAT YOU NEED IT BECAUSE...

One way you can significantly improve your ability to obtain a little bit more is to give a reason by using the magic word "because."

Yes, "because" is a powerful word that can open doors and gain concessions. In fact, the simple use of the word "because" will change how people will react to you.

In his book *Influence: Science and Practice*, Robert Cialdini describes a study performed by social scientists in 1978. In the study, researchers went to a library where there was a line of students waiting to make copies and proceeded to determine how many would let the researchers step in front of them to make copies.

94 percent of those asked agreed when they were told, "Excuse me, I have five pages. May I use the copy machine, *because I'm in a rush?*" whereas, only 60 percent granted this request when the "because" clause was dropped. To prove that the word "because" was the key factor in this startling difference, a third approach was tried, in which "because" was followed by repetitive language that did not substantively change the message (unlike the first experiment). The researcher said, "Excuse me, I have five pages. May I use the copy machine, *because I have to make some copies?*" This version yielded a 93 percent acceptance of the request.

Of course, a good reason can always help increase compliance. But don't lie about the reason. Ad copy specialists know a truthful reason is always better than a reason that is not truthful.

So when you ask for a favor or a small concession, using the word "because" is key.

THE AFTER-PARTY

You have successfully negotiated your deal. What now? Well, everyone knows that you need to document your deal in writing in order to have an enforceable contract. But is there anything else that needs to be done or should be done?

The answer is a resounding yes. Your job is not yet over. There are some subtle issues to consider during the written-documentation phase of your agreement.

This section will focus on some of the issues to remember when working on finalizing the agreement, and also on additional things that can be done as part of the negotiation process.

HAVE THEM PARTICIPATE IN WRITING IT DOWN

As you start to write up the terms of your agreement, keep in mind that it is always better to have the other side be part of this process.

As noted throughout this book, people who put things on paper are more committed. Having the other side be part of drafting the documents will keep them more committed to abiding by the agreement.

WRITING (AS OPPOSED TO FILLING IN BLANKS)

Although it is important to have the other side be involved in the drafting of the agreement, you should be the one to actually write the first draft—this allows you to control what language and terms are going to be in the agreement.

Regardless of the nature and length of the agreement, there is always something that you think of while preparing the draft that was not fully or completely addressed in the negotiations. By drafting the documents yourself you have the first shot at cleaning up any loose ends that may be left over from the negotiated deal agreement.

CREATE A CHECKLIST FOR OTHERS TO FOLLOW

After the deal has been negotiated, there generally is a brief period between the time that the deal is struck and the time that the work of complying with it begins. Before that time arrives, make sure to create a checklist for others to follow regarding the terms of the agreement.

All too often people get so caught up in the negotiation that in the end they forget all the details that need to be finalized to ensure compliance with the agreement.

One simple way to avoid things slipping through the cracks is to create a checklist of the events and things that need to happen.

For example, when I was a litigator, my office resolved cases, and we needed to make sure that the accounting was completed, all creditors were paid, the releases were signed, the courts and the witnesses were informed, and many other things. Rather than trying to remember each item, our office created a checklist that anyone could follow to determine what needed to be done to complete the process.

TEN COMMON MISTAKES MADE IN NEGOTIATION AND MEDIATION

In the course of doing thousands of mediations, I have seen many great techniques by lawyers and individual parties. I have developed and refined many of the techniques in this book. I have encouraged many strategies to play out through the process. But unfortunately, I have also seen many mistakes that collectively have cost attorneys and their clients hundreds of thousands of dollars.

This section will address some of the mistakes that are made during negotiations and mediation. Because we often learn the most from our mistakes, even though they're painful, I do not agree with former Vice President Dan Quayle, who said, "We're all capable of mistakes, but I do not care to enlighten you on the mistakes we may or may not have made." Instead, I feel like author and director Garry Marshall, who said, "It's always helpful to learn from your mistakes because then your mistakes seem worthwhile."

So let's talk about mistakes and how we can make them worthwhile.

MEDIATING OR NEGOTIATING TOO EARLY OR TOO LATE

As I mentioned to my wife recently, when I asked her to look at the sunrise and she appeared moments later just as the sun had lost some of its awe-inspiring power, "Timing is everything."

Every negotiation and every lawsuit is unique. Just as with houses, many may appear to be similar, but no two houses are exactly alike, and no two negotiations are exactly alike.

As a result, it is very difficult to identify specific rules as to when to negotiate. It's often the failure to evaluate the timing issues that can lead to what appears to be a failed mediation.

Some cases can only be mediated after a lot of work has been done; others, on the other hand, are better resolved fairly early on. The trick is for the parties and representatives to keep a watchful eye on the situation and take advantage of the limited time when it is ripe for negotiation or mediation. Several chapters in this book address the timing of when a negotiation is ripe. But in general, you need to make sure that everyone knows that they have something to lose if they do not arrive at a deal.

DISCUSSING TERMS AND DOLLARS TOO SOON

A long time ago, I attended a workshop on sales, which was discussing that 90 percent of the time should be spent on building trust, and 10 percent should be spent on selling the product. That concept has rung true for me throughout my career.

If you start to negotiate terms before you have started to build trust, the process will likely fail. Take, for example, the terrorist attack in Mumbai, India, in November of 2008. After the attack, India apparently discovered that the members of the terrorist organization were trained in Pakistan. Pakistan and India have historically fought against each other ideologically, militarily, and politically.

Pakistan's government assured India that steps had been taken to capture the terrorist group. Yet India did not believe Pakistan's assurances, and each side escalated the conflict. The reason: lack of trust.

To build trust, your actions must speak louder than your words. In litigation, the parties generally are fearful of coming to the table. They fear that they will be viewed as weak and that their gestures won't be reciprocated. Thus, you must focus on making the other side feel that they can comfortably enter negotiations and still maintain some semblance of control.

Just as most people don't fall in love overnight, most people in negotiations don't trust each other overnight. Time and commitment can be valuable allies in helping both sides feel comfortable with, and able to trust, each other. Once that trust is established, even on a limited scale, then you can talk about dollars and cents.

REFUSING TO CONCEDE THE OBVIOUS

It has been said that "he who closes his ears to the views of others shows little confidence in the integrity of his own views." In negotiations, it is crucial to maintain your own credibility through integrity. And one of the surest way to lose your credibility is to not concede points or issues that are obvious.

How people view your integrity and credibility can be critical to how the negotiation evolves. If others see you as not credible or as disingenuous, then you will have a hard time arriving at an agreement. Indeed, once you betray someone's trust or lose credibility, it is very difficult to regain that.

You lose nothing by conceding the obvious. If everybody already knows it, you may as well concede the point and gain credibility. On the other hand, you have everything to lose by insisting on the contrary.

Recently, I had a case where a dog had bitten a little girl named Megan on the lip. The dog was a plain brown mixed breed. Later in the same day of the biting, when the dog had been put away Megan's father said to Lester, the dog's owner, "I thought you put the dog away." Lester replied that he had, but the father said, "Well, I thought I saw your dog outside." Based on that fact, the defendant took the position that it was not his dog that caused the bite.

At the mediation, Lester's attorney took me aside and said, "Look, I know it is a long shot to argue that it was not our dog. Unless we find this other phantom dog, we can't credibly rely on this argument. But my client believes this is the case, so I had to argue it."

By recognizing the weakness of his argument, the attorney automatically increased his credibility. Had he not done so, and tacitly accepted the defendant's position, he would have lost credibility with the other side as well as any neutrals, such as a jury, that might evaluate the case.

BELIEVING THAT YOUR WISHES WILL CHANGE THEIR ACTIONS

Many people think that because they want to resolve a dispute, the other side will want the same thing; or they come to mediation hoping and assuming that the other side will simply see it from their perspective; that since *they* need to close the sale, the other side will agree. This can be a very costly mistake to make.

Wishing for something does not make someone else wish for the same thing or change their behavior. If that were the case, I would never be in an argument with my wife.

In fact, my wife is the perfect example of this disconnect. When I want to resolve an argument, she may not want to. No matter how hard I might try to make up, she won't give in until she is ready.

The fact of the matter is that people will act on their own schedule and according to their own sensibilities. No matter how much you want to change that, you can't.

DEMANDING TOTAL CAPITULATION

Some people will come to mediation with the sole goal of winning. They do not give an inch unless they are forced to do so; they treat negotiations as an "I win, so you must lose; and if I lose, then you have won" scenario. They will demand total capitulation and will never leave a face-saving way out for the other side.

Many times, the party that perceives it has the greatest power will assume that it can demand total capitulation. Many settlements, however, are lost exactly because the party with leverage and power attempts to dictate *all* the terms.

This tactic can, and often does, backfire. No one likes to be forced to do anything against their will. No one likes to be threatened. In fact, when threatened, people will often go out of their way to do the opposite of what is demanded. As Niccolò Machiavelli once said, "I consider it a mark of great prudence in a man to abstain from threats or any contemptuous expressions, for neither of these weaken the enemy, but threats make him more cautious, and the other excites his hatred, and a desire to revenge himself."

And a final reason that demanding total capitulation can backfire very easily, is that the other side knows it has only two choices: to accept defeat or to fight and *probably* suffer defeat—and the latter option usually looks like the better deal.

In a recent medical malpractice case, the plaintiff sued a doctor for committing malpractice against her father. By the time the case got to mediation, both parties had conducted a substantial amount of investigation. The defendant had been arguing all along that, although something may have happened in the operating room, his actions did not cause harm to the patient—and it appeared that he was probably right.

However, the defendant refused to give the plaintiff any way out except to admit that her action was filed frivolously, which the plaintiff refused to do. The plaintiff's attorney tried to help find a solution that would allow his client to gracefully exit the litigation. However, the defendant insisted on an all-or-nothing proposition of dismissal or trial. At the end of the mediation, the parties agreed to arbitrate the matter before a retired judge for a binding result. Four weeks later, I received a call from the plaintiff's attorney telling me the arbitrator had awarded his client $125,000. The plaintiff had won the case.

When you back the other side into a corner with no way out, you might just find yourself trapped there also.

NEGOTIATING AND MEDIATING WITHOUT THE NECESSARY PARTIES

It makes sense that one wants to find the proper parties to negotiate with. But you would be surprised at how many times parties will enter mediation just to find that all the necessary parties are not present. The net result is that the matter cannot get resolved and everyone has just wasted a lot of time and money.

Take the case of potential medical malpractice and nursing home negligence. The nursing home and the plaintiff's family started to negotiate. But any time any discussion about the facts arose, either the nursing home was claiming that the injuries arose at the hospital, or the medical records clearly identified that the hospital had more involvement.

The parties had hoped to simply resolve their aspect of the case. The plaintiff realized, however, that if the nursing home resolved its dispute, the hospital could easily point the finger at the nursing home. And the nursing home realized that in order to have a chance of arriving at a mutually satisfactory agreement, the hospital needed to participate and contribute.

The road may be paved with good intentions, but without all the necessary parties it still may lead to nowhere.

NOT GETTING IT IN WRITING

The failure to get the agreement in writing is probably one of the biggest mistakes a negotiator can make. No matter what the deal or agreement, you should always get something in writing.

As noted earlier, *Jerry Maguire* is the perfect example of why you must get it in writing. Many people will end a mediation with an oral agreement. They are tired and want to go home. But a failure to get something in writing risks that all the good work you accomplished may be undone by simple buyer's remorse, which is why I insist that some form of written document be executed by all parties.

This is especially true in litigation, where mediation often is a zero-sum game—the more you get, the less I keep. Many times the parties feel very strongly about their version of the case. At the end of the day, they may be unhappy with the result but would rather have a resolution than risk a coin toss at trial. However, given enough time and enough stories of friends of friends who received millions in damages from a mere splinter, they may change their minds.

In one particularly difficult case, the plaintiff had claimed that she had been discriminated against because of her race. The mediation had taken all day, and both sides had compromised substantially, only to end up $5,000 apart. Neither party would budge. Neither party entertained further offers. The defendant assumed that, having gotten this far, the plaintiff would take their last offer since it was only $5,000 away from the plaintiff's final demand. In many other cases they might have been right, but this plaintiff had repeatedly told the other side that she believed in the principle and would fight "all the way to the Supreme Court." I was in the middle of trying to talk with the defendants about the risks they were taking by drawing a line in the sand over such a small amount, when the plaintiff's attorney informed me that his client, like Elvis, had left the building, without so much as a word of goodbye.

I ran after her but couldn't find her in the lobby, so I ran back into the conference room and told the defendant that I couldn't find her. The defendant said, "OK, fine, I'll pay the extra $5,000 to have resolution. See if you can get her back." I ran out again, but this time into the parking lot, where I just caught her and told her that we should at least discuss the issue and that the defendant was willing to meet her demands.

We walked back to my office. On the way back, she agreed to the deal. I prepared my short form agreement and asked everyone to sign. But the defendant said, "I want my formal documents to be signed, so let's have them drafted and then we can sign that later. I would like to get on the road." I refused to allow that to happen and insisted that we sign some papers, even limited ones, to memorialize the deal, and we signed my two-page agreement. The very next day, the plaintiff called to tell me she did not want to agree anymore; now she wanted $20,000 more. Ultimately, the parties were able to go to court to enforce the settlement—and the only thing that saved the deal was that small, two-page short form agreement.

Always get it in writing.

RUSHING THE PROCESS; BEING IMPATIENT

Negotiations take time—hours, days, weeks, months, even years. When I asked my wife to marry me, it was only after years of negotiating, concessions, and preparation.

A negotiator with 30 years' experience, Robert J. Conover explained the importance of patience when he wrote, "Patience is more than biding your time. Patience is listening when you feel like telling; empathizing when you feel like giving up; talking when you feel like screaming; hesitating when you feel like pouncing; and compromising when you feel like asserting. Patience does not come easy. You must train yourself in its subtleties, in its measure, in its timing, in its influence, and in its wisdom. Patience is a virtue possessed by all good negotiators."

The negotiation and mediation process is just as important as the substance, if not more important. People do not just instantly understand the other side's positions. It takes time to understand the issues. It takes time to evaluate risks and benefits. It takes even more time to evaluate the other's strengths and weaknesses. And finally, it takes time to change the other side's perceptions and expectations.

Most importantly, time allows the mind to adjust to a new reality. Even the smallest change can be difficult to accept. The bigger the negotiation, the more time it could take.

Take the way humans react to a change in temperature. When you put your hand in a really hot Jacuzzi or bowl of water, you will instantly pull back because it is too painful to bear. However, if you put your hand in a bowl of tepid water and then take the time to heat the water up slowly, your body gets used to the heat. In fact, research has shown that we tolerate more pain if the pain is increased slowly.

The same is true for negotiations. Don't worry about the clock. Worry about what you have learned and how far you must go to obtain resolution.

ASSUMING "THIS IS MY FINAL OFFER" REALLY IS THE FINAL OFFER

Have you ever been in a negotiation where someone said, "This is my final offer," just to make another one shortly thereafter? Well, if you haven't, you will. When hearing this phrase, take it with a grain of salt—many times, the "final offer" is just a negotiating ploy.

Accepting a "final offer" at face value implies that the other person is telling the truth. Some negotiation researchers, however, have suggested that lying is acceptable in negotiations; Professor James J. White even asserts that misleading the other side is the very "essence of negotiation."

If you're presented with a bottom line or a final offer, you have to test whether it, in fact, is the *actual* bottom line. What if the person making the offer subscribes to Professor White's philosophy? Only when you are convinced that the "final offer" truly is just that should you consider how to react to it.

TALKING TOO MUCH

Too many negotiators feel that being a negotiator means they must talk all the time. One of the United States' most famous advisors, Ann Landers, said it best when she said, "The trouble with talking too fast is you may say something you haven't thought of yet."

When you are talking, you are giving away information. Even if you are making idle conversation, be careful what you say. How many times have you heard some form of the phrase "They will use what I say against me." I can guarantee you that no one ever says, "They will use what I hear against me."

One of the most common mistakes in negotiation is talking too much and listening too little. Listening is a way of controlling the negotiations. You learn by listening. Which is why no teacher will tell her class, "You kids aren't talking enough. Stop listening and talk." As stated earlier, information is power, and when you are talking, the only thing you are doing is giving away information.

Learn to ask good questions to get the other side talking. By listening, you will create a better rapport, and when the other person starts to like you more, he will be more open to your ideas when it's your turn to speak.

Albert Einstein once explained the keys to success as a simple equation: "If A equals success, then the formula is A equals X plus Y and Z, with X being work, Y play, and Z keeping your mouth shut."

ABOUT THE AUTHOR

Steven G. Mehta is one of California's premier award-winning attorney mediators thanks to his work in helping resolve disputes in a variety of types of civil litigation. Steve has been successfully mediating complex cases since 1999. He has been repeatedly selected by his peers as a "SuperLawyer" in the field of mediation and has been selected as one of the "Best Lawyers in America" in the field of mediation. His unique ability to understand the human process and the complex emotional issues involved in negotiations enables him to effectively assist the parties in obtaining the best possible results during mediation.

Steve is well known and respected as being a fair and neutral mediator who works hard at trying to obtain a favorable resolution for both sides. Lawyers who have worked with Steve have described him as "knowledgeable, patient, and creative," "outstanding," a "very capable mediator," a "miracle worker," and as having a "friendly and professional demeanor."

Steve has taught thousands of lawyers and businesspeople to negotiate better. His courses are highly sought after and often sold out.

He is the coauthor of the California State Bar's book *Opening a Law Office*.

Steve specializes in resolving very difficult and emotionally complex or charged cases. He can be reached through his website at www.stevemehta.com.

ADDITIONAL READING AND RESOURCES

Aubuchon, Norbert. *Anatomy of Persuasion.* New York: AMACOM, 1997.

Beckwith, Harry. *Selling the Invisible: A Field Guide to Modern Marketing.* New York: Warner Books, 1997.

Beyond Intractability: More Constructive Approaches to Destructive Conflict. 28 March 2009. <http://www.beyondintractability.org/essay/trust_mediation/>.

Cialdini, Robert B. *Influence: Science and Practice* (5th Edition). Boston: Allyn & Bacon, 2008.

Cohen, Raymond. *Negotiating Across Cultures: Communication Obstacles in International Diplomacy.* Washington, D.C.: United States Institute of Peace, 1991.

Covey, Stephen R. *The Seven Habits of Highly Effective People: Restoring the Character Ethic.* New York: Simon and Schuster, 1989.

Dawson, Roger. *Secrets of Power Negotiating for Salespeople.* Franklin Lakes: Career Press, 1999.

Donaldson, Michael C., and Mimi Donaldson. *Negotiating for Dummies.* Foster City: IDG Books, 1996.

Fayerweather, J., and A. Kapoor. "Strategy and Negotiation for the International Corporation." Sales & Marketing Management, May (1992): 64-70.

Fine, Debra. *The Fine Art of Small Talk: How to Start a Conversation, Keep It Going, Build Networking Skills—and Leave a Positive Impression!* New York: Hyperion, 2005.

Fisher, Roger. *Getting to Yes: Negotiating Agreements Without Giving In.* New York: Penguin Books, 1983.

Greene, Robert. *48 Laws of Power.* New York: Viking, 1998.
Greene, Robert. *The Art of Seduction.* New York: Penguin Books, 2001.
Hogan, Kevin. *The Science of Influence: How to Get Anyone to Say "Yes" in 8 Minutes or Less!* New York: Wiley, 2004.
Humes, James C. *Nixon's Ten Commandments of Leadership and Negotiation: His Guiding Principles of Statecraft.* New York: Touchstone, 1998.
Kopelman, S., and A. S. Thompson. "The Three Faces of Eve: Strategic Displays of Positive, Negative & Neutral Emotions in Negotiations." Organizational Behavior and Human Decision Processes 99 (2006): 81-101.
Lesikar, Raymond V., and Marie E. Flatley. *Basic Business Communication Skills for Empowering the Internet Generation.* New York: McGraw-Hill/Irwin, 2004.
Levinson, Jay Conrad. *Guerrilla Negotiating: Unconventional Weapons and Tactics to Get What You Want.* New York: John Wiley, 1999.
Lieberman, David J. *How to Change Anybody: Proven Techniques to Reshape Anyone's Attitude, Behavior, Feelings, or Beliefs.* Boston: St. Martin's Griffin, 2005.
Mackay, Harvey B. *Swim with the Sharks Without Being Eaten Alive.* New York: Harper Business Essentials, 2005.
Malhotra, Deepak, and Max Bazerman. *Negotiation Genius: How to Overcome Obstacles and Achieve Brilliant Results at the Bargaining Table and Beyond.* New York: Bantam, 2007.
McGinty, Sarah Myers. *Power Talk: Using Language to Build Authority and Influence.* New York: Warner Business Books, 2001.
Mills, Harry. *Artful Persuasion: How to Command Attention, Change Minds, and Influence People.* New York: AMACOM, 2000.
Moore, Don A. "Use Deadlines for Powerful Negotiations—HBS Working Knowledge." HBS Working Knowledge—Faculty Research at Harvard Business School. 28 January 2009. <http://hbswk.hbs.edu/archive/4354.html>.
Mortensen, Kurt W., and Robert G. Allen. *Maximum Influence: The 12 Universal Laws of Power Persuasion.* New York: AMACOM, 2004.
Nance, Jef. *Conquering Deception.* New York: Irvin Benham Group, 2001.
Niven, David. *Simple Secrets of Love.* San Francisco: Harper, 2004.
Reilly, Leo. *How to Outnegotiate Anyone (Even a Car Dealer!).* Holbrook, Mass: B. Adams, 1994.
"Robert J. Conover—Master Mediation Negotiator/Claims Rep." 12 March 2009. <http://www.rjcnegotiator.citymaker.com/page/page/1785190.htm>.

Scott, Susan. *Fierce Conversations: Achieving Success at Work and in Life, One Conversation at a Time.* New York: Viking, 2002.

Shell, G. Richard. *Bargaining for Advantage: Negotiation Strategies for Reasonable People.* New York: Penguin (Non-Classics), 2000.

Sims, Jonathan. "The Ideal Location for Negotiation: An Alternative View: by Jonathan Sims." The Negotiator Magazine. 28 March 2009. <http://www.negotiatormagazine.com/article290_1.html>.

Stone, Douglas, Bruce Patton, and Sheila Heen. *Difficult Conversations.* New York: Penguin Books, 1999.

Ury, William. *Getting Past No: Negotiating Your Way from Confrontation to Cooperation.* New York: Bantam Books, 1993.

Ury, William. *The Power of a Positive No: How to Say No and Still Get to Yes.* New York: Bantam, 2007.

White, James J. "Machiavelli and the Bar: Ethical Limitations on Lying in Negotiation." Law and Social Inquiry 5 (2006).

Printed in the United States
148814LV00002B/4/P